TOUCHING TH

CHRIS THORPE is a parish priest in Shifnal, Shropshire, in the Diocese of Lichfield.

JAKE LEVER is an artist and teacher, based in Cheltenham, Gloucestershire. He has exhibited widely in galleries, churches and festivals.

Using the material in this book, they have led quiet days in cathedrals and local churches and have created 'sanctuary space' at Greenbelt Festival.

Pippa and John
with all good wishes,

Chris Thorpe

TOUCHING
THE
SACRED

Art and prayer to inspire worship

Words by
CHRIS THORPE

Images by
JAKE LEVER

CANTERBURY
PRESS
Norwich

© in the text Chris Thorpe 2010
© in the illustrations Jake Lever 2010

First published in 2010 by the Canterbury Press Norwich
Editorial office
13–17 Long Lane,
London, EC1A 9PN, UK

Canterbury Press is an imprint of
Hymns Ancient and Modern Ltd (a registered charity)
St Mary's Works, 13A Hellesdon Park Road,
Norwich, NR6 5DR, UK

www.scm-canterburypress.co.uk

Bible readings are from the New Revised Standard Version
of the Bible, copyright 1989 by the Division of Christian
Education of the National Council of the Churches of Christ
in the USA. Used by permission. All rights reserved.

Psalms and canticles are from *Common Worship: Services and
Prayers for the Church of England* copyright © 2000,
The Archbishops' Council and are reproduced by permission.

British Library Cataloguing in Publication data

A catalogue record for this book is available
from the British Library

978 1 84825 024 6

Designed and typeset by Vera Brice

Printed and bound in Great Britain by
CPI Antony Rowe, Chippenham, Wiltshire

CONTENTS

Dedicated to

Sarah, Sophie and Jake

and

Gillian, Joseph and Toby

SETTING THE SCENE

HOW TO USE
THIS BOOK

These acts of worship may be used by individuals, small groups or in larger settings as frameworks for silence and reflection. They have been used in church services, in quiet days, retreats, and to conclude small group discussions. They take the form of short 'offices', offering psalms, short biblical readings, reflections, silence, music, and prayers of recognition and intercession. All of the images and words are on the CD and may be used to create service sheets and for digital projection.

INDIVIDUAL
REFLECTION

As an individual, the images and reflections may be used as the basis of a quiet time, a day away or retreat. The choice of image will be important and it is worth listening to which of the themes speaks to you as you look through the contents page. Do you want to explore your sense of calling or your giftedness? Are you working with suffering or difficult questions? Are you looking to discover your own inner creativity? You might like to select an image to focus your reflection, and to print off an A4 colour copy to be used as an icon for your prayer time. For me, the images have revealed themselves at a deeper and deeper level, as I have given them time to sink in. A possible structure for a quiet morning would be:

* To use the prayer of stillness and the psalm to create the context to approach the image, and then to spend ten minutes or so simply 'being' with the picture, taking it in, letting its features become apparent to you. It might be worth having a notepad to record your impressions for later.

* To read the Reflection, as you re-look at the

image. Some of the thoughts may connect, or open up new avenues of thought, while others may not be meaningful for you. The reflection is not meant to be proscriptive, and you may be taken in another direction entirely!

∗   You may like to give some time for this to sink in, a walk, a longer silence of perhaps half an hour, a piece of music, just to let some of the impressions and reflections settle.

∗   Returning to the image, the Invocation takes you back into the heart of the reflection, and may then be followed by the Prayers of Recognition. These are intended to be taken slowly, to allow the themes to be rooted, recognized in our own lives, connecting with our own experiences.

∗   On an individual retreat you might like to respond to the image in a creative way, by writing a poem, a prayer, or a reflection of your own; or to draw or paint or craft your own piece in clay to say how this has connected with your life, your experiences.

∗   Drawing the quiet time together you might like to offer your journal, prayers, poem, etc. to God and to use the final prayer to bring the time to a close.

SMALL GROUP
REFLECTIONS

If you are a house group leader, or run an Emmaus or Alpha course, and are looking for a short act of worship to conclude an evening, you may like to choose one of the images and reflections. The short 'office' will take about 30 minutes and can provide a powerful stillness at the end of a word-filled discussion evening.

If you are planning a group quiet morning or a shared retreat, the images and reflections can be used in a similar way to an individual retreat and much of the above will be relevant. You might like to choose a selection of images from different sections of the book, or to do a mini-series from one section. We have found that less is often more when it comes to using the images, and we tend to use three images as a basis for a quiet day, taking care not to overload people with too many at once.

A key choice can be the use of projected images and words, and/or individual printed cards for reflection. If you are using a data projector it is essential that the 'technology' does not dominate the scene, and great care should be taken in setting up and being completely sure of how the projector and computer work! While the projected image, by its very size, can provide a good visual centre for the group, there may be times when you want people to be able to go off on their own to reflect, and it is then that it may be good to have a printed copy for each person. It also allows people to take something away with them at the end of the event and to go on reflecting on it.

In setting the scene for worship we endeavour to show that the space is set aside in some way. Sometimes we have asked people to remove their shoes before entering the worship space to emphasize that 'this is holy ground' and to raise the sense of expectation of an encounter with the sacred. The most bland of rooms can be transformed with the use of tea-lights on the window sills and by clearing out the furniture.

LARGER-SCALE EVENTS   We have also used the material with much larger groups, whole congregations and, at the Greenbelt Festival, with hundreds of people at a time. On this scale the data projector is clearly the best means of making the image available to people. Often on this larger scale there may need to be more than one projector and the screens need to be positioned to allow people to see the image clearly. There will also need to be some sound system to ensure that people can hear. Again the technology needs to be as unobtrusive as possible and if possible it should be controlled by someone other than the worship leader.

For the larger event we tend to use PowerPoint to create a presentation of both the image and words for a service. Over time we have tended to put less and less words on the screen, and allow more time for people to reflect on the image. As a guide, we now use just enough words on screen to enable people to understand where they are in the structure of the service, and to respond where appropriate. Some sample PowerPoint presentations can be found on the CD accompanying the book. We do however find that people ask for something to take away with them, and thought can be given to how this might be achieved. A printed copy of the Invocation section can sometimes act as a 'summary' for people to keep after the event.

We have always tried to create a feeling of intimacy even in the large venues by using material drapes to 'soften' the space and to subdue the lighting. In a darkened space it is important to be aware of health and safety issues if there is any movement, for example if people come up for anointing or for prayer. Make sure there are no stray wires for people to trip over, that there is adequate light for people to see where they are going and clear passageways.

PLANNING AN EVENT Whatever the size of the event, the following notes may be helpful to leaders in their preparation.

IMAGES All of these liturgies have been inspired by reflection on these icon-like images by Jake Lever. The use of art in spirituality opens up completely new avenues of thought, uses different parts of our brains, and provokes a response. The images are available in full colour on the CD and may be projected onto a screen or printed as individual A4 sheets or postcards as a focus for prayer and contemplation.

CONTEXT   The liturgies are intended to help people to reflect deeply on their personal faith, so time given to arranging an intimate setting will be valuable. Seating, lighting, shape and ambience of the room will all be important. Attention to posture and stillness will allow people to enter into the worship more fully. Provide floor cushions (and prayer stools if you have them) as well as chairs, and invite people to find a position that is comfortable for them.

PACE   If you are using the liturgies as an act of worship, the basic service will take about 30 minutes in its simplest form. The liturgy is intended to be spacious, taken slowly and with pauses to allow the images room to live and breathe. It is good to hear a variety of voices, so it may be possible to invite people to participate in reading different sections.

SILENCE   Silence is the key to the whole liturgy, but the leader may need to gauge how much silence a particular group can cope with. Many people are completely unused to silence, and will feel uncomfortable at first, so it is essential to introduce the silence, to help people to know what is going to happen. Some people will need a question to take with them into the silence, something to think about; others may be comfortable with a word of scripture – 'be still and know that I am God', or the Jesus prayer, 'Lord Jesus Christ, Son of God, have mercy on me', or perhaps a phrase related to the theme. We suggest that a silence be at least five minutes long, building up to eight or ten minutes as people become more familiar with it. As the leader it is important that you are not afraid of the silence, and that you aren't panicked into ending it early!

RESPONSES   The responses are in bold type, and there are opportunities where these may be said or sung, or replaced with a familiar Taizé, Iona or other chant or chorus.

REFLECTION   There is no single interpretation of these images, far from it, they will speak differently to each person who reflects upon them. The interpretations and reflections offered in these liturgies are merely a starting point and leaders may wish to prepare their own words of reflection, or invite others to comment about what they see in the image.

MUSIC   The use of music in the times of reflection is intended to offer yet another 'way in' to the silence; like the images, music speaks to another part of our selves. We have found that less familiar music can add to the creative experience for people, taking them into unfamiliar places. Pieces by James Macmillan, Karl Jenkins, Avo Pärt, Erkki-Sven Tuur, John Tavener, Gyorgy Ligeti, as well as more ancient music by Byrd, Palestrina, Hildegaard von Bingen, Tallis, have all been good. Music from Taizé and Iona can give a reflective feel too. Just one caveat – be aware of music with words as sometimes the words can get in the way for some people.

PRAYERS OF RECOGNITION   This section is particularly intended to allow people to make a personal connection with the theme of the liturgy, to take it into our own lives and experience. It is especially important not to rush this, but to give space for people to absorb the words before responding.

PRAYERS OF INTERCESSION   The leader may want to offer a first prayer, or prompt someone to pray, to give permission for people to speak. After having had a very personal focus to the reflections, it is good if these prayers can be outward focused, offered for the world.

ENDINGS   It is important to have a proper ending for a service
– the final prayer will often be the signal for this, and
will give permission for people to leave. In some
settings, if there is scope after the liturgy, it can be
good to play further music and allow people time to
continue to be still while others leave quietly.

INTRODUCTION TO
THE IMAGES

ANGEL HANDS These images were made for my friend Chris Thorpe
for his contemplation in solitude on Bardsey Island.
The source for these works was a group of twelfth-
century angels painted as Romanesque frescoes,
transferred from the tiny hilltop churches of
northern Spain to the Palau National in Barcelona.
The elegance, subtlety and poise of these hand
gestures struck me as deeply inspirational; these
hands seemed to belong to beings from another
world. Fingers point playfully down from the
heavens or guide us onwards in our search. The
all-seeing eyes of the seraphs pierce these palms like
wounds, watchers of both the human and the divine.
Rough seas meant that I never reached Bardsey to
hand over the finished prints to Chris, but they
turned up instead in a busy vicarage, accompanying
him on a different kind of journey.

CHRIST HANDS These were the very first images I made after
discovering the process of intaglio printmaking
using simple plates made of card. Finding myself in
the Sainsbury's Wing of the National Gallery,
London, I was magnetically drawn to the hands of
Christ – limp, lacerated, torn and twisted through
crucifixion. Perhaps for the first time in my life I was
in touch with my own vulnerability, and these frail
hands resonated with me very deeply. Created by
violent cutting and stabbing of printing plates, the
wounds are fresh, open and raw. Some wounds have
been gilded as cracks once were on broken china. In
Christ the 'wounded healer' we see the possibility of
pain transformed.

xx TOUCHING THE SACRED

MAGI HANDS The image that is the basis for many of the Magi hands is an ancient American Indian sculpted hand from the first to fourth century AD, found in Ohio. I wanted to use an image outside of the Christian West, something that could hint at the universal dimension of human experience and Divine revelation. I was drawn to its simplicity and it struck me that it possessed a timeless, primordial quality that chimed with the wisdom of the Magi. I imagined the hands of the three magi as broad and solid, rooted in ancient knowledge. The Magi stretch out their ancient, leathery hands like creased maps charting long journeys. The experience of rough, difficult terrain has been etched into the palms of these generous astronomers, star-led chieftains radiant with lunar wisdom.

JESTER HANDS – The Holy Fool is the risk-taker, truth-teller, the free
THE HOLY FOOL spirit who flouts convention and goes against the tide. He or she challenges and questions, disarming the mighty and powerful with subversive, outrageous foolery. The Holy Fool mocks the idiocy of the world, pointing to the upside-down nature of the Kingdom of God where 'the first shall be last' and where the wisdom of the world is foolishness in the eyes of God. These hands, etched with silver ink on black paper, tickle and prod mischievously from the dark margins of our world. Nudging us gently out of our comfort zone, these holy jesters invite us to risk, dance, struggle and love.

Jake Lever

MICHAELMAS
Watchers and Holy Ones

Angel Hands
Exploring Our Calling

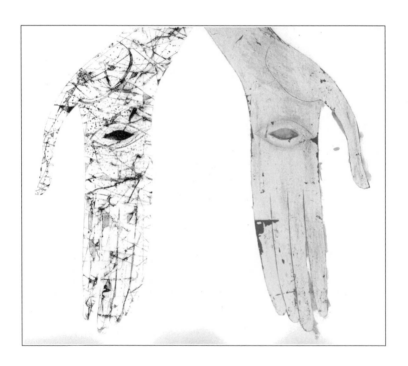

INTRODUCTION

Jake Lever offered these angel hands for me to take
into a time of sabbatical reflection some years ago.
Their simple beauty and mystery provoked me to
consider how I could relate to these angels, these
messengers of divinity. I had never thought about their
meaning or purpose, it was unfamiliar territory for me.
Starting with scripture, I struggled to discern the different character of each hand and the angel's purpose or
gift. I found in them different personalities, connecting
with human experience in different ways. Finding
words to address each angel led me, as I suppose
they intended, into a conversation with God.

The feast of St Michael and All Angels, 29 September, is
a good time to introduce these angel hands and they
span the whole season of All Saints, Remembrance
Tide, and Advent through an exploration of the theme
of our vocation, our calling. Angels have been seen as
heralds of good tidings, messengers of God's judgement, as preparing the way of the Lord. *Angelos* come
in many different forms, from human beings to winged
beings. They have bridged the gap between earth and
heaven.

I have sought to root each reflection in a biblical
passage, to pick up some of the major functions and
roles of the angelic host. The angels reflect something
of the character of God, each a different facet of God.
These liturgies may be used individually as the heart of
a service of the word, or as the act of worship following
a discussion group. They may also be grouped to provide the framework for a retreat or quiet day, alternat-
ing each office with a time of silence, and times of
creative writing, art or response in other ways.

Michael, the Archangel, is known to us from the Revelation to St John, where he led the cosmic battle against evil, and today we celebrate him as a champion of social action for the justice of God. **Wrestler,** the unknown assailant of Jacob, the stranger who wrestled with him till daybreak, bringer of struggle and blessing, inspires us to wrestle and struggle with our faith and doubts. **Watchers,** the guardian angels who look on the face of God and watch over each of us, are those spoken of by Jesus as affirming the dignity of each human person. Today we share their gaze in the prayer of contemplation, the call to be still. **Raphael,** the unrecognized companion in the apocryphal book of Tobit, appears as a stranger on the road, whose touch brings healing and new energy to the exhausted travellers. Perhaps we can become more alert as we meet strangers in our everyday lives; we may be entertaining angels unawares. **Seraphs** are to be found in the story of the calling of the prophet Isaiah, who was overwhelmed by the majesty of God and by his own inadequacy. The Seraph in his vision touched his mouth to empower him to speak. When we feel that we have little to offer, we need that same reassurance and empowerment. **Sanctus** reminds us of the angelic choir who constantly sing before God's throne, 'Holy, Holy, Holy Lord, God of power and might'. Their call to worship allows us to value the unresolved questions of our faith. **Gabriel,** the herald of the incarnation, comes to Mary and tells her that the Holy Spirit will overshadow her and that she will bear a child who will be the saviour of his people. The Archangel shows us 'heaven in ordinary', and points us to our own vocation, of the Word made flesh in us.

MICHAEL

– the call to radical engagement

Unfreezing our fear, unlocking our compassion, entering the fray

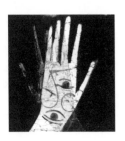

OPENING PRAYER

O God, who calls us to stand
circle our hearts,
centre our minds,
still our bodies,
be present to us now.
Amen.

CANTICLE
Psalm 18.31–36

As for God, his way is perfect; the word of the Lord
is tried in the fire;
he is a shield to all who trust in him.

**For who is God but the Lord,
and who is the rock except our God?**

It is God who girds me about with strength
and makes my way perfect.

**He makes my feet like hinds' feet
so that I tread surely on the heights.**

He teaches my hands to fight
and my arms to bend a bow of bronze.

**You have given me the shield of your salvation;
your right hand upholds me and your grace has
made me great.**

**Glory to the Father, and to the Son,
and to the Holy Spirit;
as it was in the beginning, is now
and shall be for ever. Amen.**

SCRIPTURE
READING
The Revelation of
St John 12.7–9

And war broke out in heaven; Michael and his angels fought against the dragon. The dragon and his angels fought back, but they were defeated, and there was no longer any place for them in heaven. The great dragon was thrown down, that ancient serpent, who is called the Devil and Satan, the deceiver of the whole world – he was thrown down to the earth, and his angels were thrown down with him.

REFLECTION

Look at the strength of these hands, facing two ways, straight strong fingers, there is a sense of commanding presence, a 'this far and no further' kind of directness. There are choices to be made, sides to be taken. These hands speak of radical engagement, a daring to stand and be counted in the company of freedom and justice.

In a time when we have turned to 'gentle Jesus meek and mild' and found him wanting, these hands remind us of Jesus overturning the tables in the Temple, whipping out the money changers and extortionists. They remind us that we are to be the 'church militant here upon earth', that there are choices to be made, battles to be fought, causes to be won.

Michael can inspire us to set up credit unions to stand against the loan sharks, to plant trees in the city to break up the concrete, to make wonderful pictures in the face of war, to design sustainable buildings that will preserve our environment. These hands lead us into the heart of the conflict, but these are not clenched fists, ready to fight and to hurt, these strong hands are open, even to nails.

MUSIC   *A time of meditation*

SILENCE   We take into the silence the people who have stood
up for us, who have made an impact on something
that matters. We think of the issues that we face, the
stand that we might be called to take, the ways that
we can engage that will make a
difference.

INVOCATION TO   O Michael, divine champion,
MICHAEL   hero of heaven, instrument of judgement,
you who hear the cries of God's people,
the hunger of the poor,
the oppression of the weak,
you who see the tortured prisoner,
the abused child,
you who fought the dragon and his angels:
arise,
come to our aid,
embolden us to speak out with prophetic voice,
empower us to act in the name of Justice.

PRAYERS OF   We bring to God, all that is fearful in us, all that
RECOGNITION   paralyses and prevents us, and we let it go.

Cantor: Goodness is stronger than evil
All: **Love is stronger than hate**

We bring to God all that is indifferent, all that is
hardened and unmoved in us, and we let it go.

Cantor: Goodness is stronger than evil
All: **Love is stronger than hate**

We bring to God all that crowds out our care, our
busyness and preoccupation, and we let it go.

Cantor: Goodness is stronger than evil
All: **Love is stronger than hate**

And because we are called to act, we bring to God all that moves us, our compassion and understanding, and we offer it.

Cantor: Light is stronger than darkness
All: Life is stronger than death

We bring to God our courage, our strength and our determination, and we offer it.

Cantor: Light is stronger than darkness
All: Life is stronger than death

We bring to God our freedom, our ability, our gifted-ness, and we offer it.

Cantor: Light is stronger than darkness
All: Life is stronger than death

PRAYERS OF   *A time of open prayer when we can bring to God*
INTERCESSION *people and situations that we care about*

After each intercession
Let us pray to the Lord
Lord have mercy

CLOSING PRAYER   **O God,**
enlist us in your company of freedom,
recruit us to the cause of justice,
unfreeze our fear,
undo our indifference,
unlock our compassion,
enable our hands to work and act and move for you
who are in the heart of the conflict.
Amen.

(Responses based on the words of Archbishop Desmond Tutu)

WRESTLER

– the call to grapple with the questions

The importance of struggle, doubts and questions for human maturity and depth

OPENING PRAYER

O God who wrestles with us,
circle our hearts,
centre our minds,
still our bodies,
be present to us now.
Amen.

CANTICLE
A Song of Humility

Come, let us return to the Lord
who has torn us and will heal us.

**God has stricken us
and will bind up our wounds.**

After two days, he will revive us,
and on the third day will raise us up,
that we may live in his presence.

**Let us strive to know the Lord;
his appearing is as sure as the sunrise.**

He will come to us like the showers,
like the spring rains that water the earth.

**Glory to the Father, and to the Son,
and to the Holy Spirit;
as it was in the beginning, is now
and shall be for ever. Amen.**

SCRIPTURE
READING
Genesis 32.24–28

Jacob was left alone; and a man wrestled with him until daybreak. When the man saw that he did not prevail against Jacob, he struck him on the hip socket; and Jacob's hip was put out of joint as he wrestled with him. Then he said, 'Let me go, for the day is breaking.' But Jacob said, 'I will not let you go, unless you bless me.' So he said to him, 'What is your name?' And he said, 'Jacob.' Then the man said, 'You shall no longer be called Jacob, but Israel, for you have striven with God and with humans, and have prevailed.'

REFLECTION

All through the night, these hands have wrestled and struggled. Now, for a moment before parting, they are still. The golden translucence of the angel, the white hand of Jacob. The struggle has been relentless, exhausting, costly; it has left Jacob wounded. Nevertheless he has hung on, and in hanging on, he has prevailed, he has been blessed.

Struggle and blessing have been at the heart of Israel's history. They have been a people of struggle – struggle against oppression, invasion, exile, struggle to fashion their faith in a way that holds true to God and to their experience. For us too a faith without struggle cannot be real faith. Often we argue and struggle with God. Like Jesus in the wilderness and in the garden of Gethsemane, our faith is forged through struggle, it is tested in the heat, tested to breaking point, but strengthened if we can hold on.

And it's not always about resolving the struggle, winning, defeating our adversary and sorting everything out. Often questions will remain unanswered, situations remain unresolved. Perhaps this hand can encourage us that even in messy and unwinnable struggles, it is enough to engage fully, with all our hearts and minds and strength, to hang on in there and not to give up.

MUSIC   *A time of meditation*

SILENCE   We think of the struggles we have known in our
lives: with God, with others and with ourselves.

INVOCATION TO   O Wrestler,
GABRIEL   contending with us until daybreak,
holding us in the grip of your argument,
grappling with our questions and doubts,
you who strive to deepen us through struggle,
and strengthen us through adversity:
hold on to us now
in that fierce love
that will never let us go.
Bless us, as you name us,
as those who have prevailed.

PRAYERS OF   We bring to God all our false certainties, religious
RECOGNITION   platitudes and trite answers, and we let them go.

Cantor: God has stricken us
All: And will bind up our wounds

We bring to God all that is comfortable and self-
satisfied in us, and we let it go.

Cantor: God has stricken us
All: And will bind up our wounds

We bring to God the times we have avoided the
struggle, taken the line of least resistance, colluded,
and we let them go.

Cantor: God has stricken us
All: And will bind up our wounds

And because we believe that God does bless us, we
bring to God our questions and doubts and uncer-
tainties, and we offer them.

Cantor: Bless us as you name us
All: As those who have prevailed

We bring to God all that we find hard to deal with,
tasks, relationships, feelings, and we offer them.

Cantor: Bless us as you name us
All: As those who have prevailed

We bring to God all the messy, unwinnable struggles
and adversities that we face, and we offer them.

Cantor: Bless us as you name us
All: As those who have prevailed

PRAYERS OF   *A time of open prayer when we can bring to God*
INTERCESSION   *people and situations that we care about*

After each intercession
Let us pray to the Lord
Lord have mercy

CLOSING PRAYER   **O God of Jacob, struggle with us**
through the dark nights of our questioning,
hang on to us when we lose hold of you.
Cripple our false certainties,
disable our selfishness,
that though we come stumbling and limping
we may come to see you face to face.
Amen.

WATCHER

– the call to be still

Don't just do something, sit there! Contemplative prayer, the gaze of love

OPENING PRAYER O God who calls us to watch,
circle our hearts ,
centre our minds,
still our bodies,
be present to us now.
Amen.

CANTICLE When he has turned to the prayer of the destitute
Psalm 102.18–23 and has not despised their plea,

**This shall be written for those that come after,
and a people yet unborn shall praise the Lord.**

For he has looked down from his holy height;
from the heavens he beheld the earth,

**That he might hear the sighings of the prisoner
and set free those condemned to die;**

That the name of the Lord may be proclaimed in Zion
and his praises in Jerusalem,

**When peoples are gathered together
and kingdoms also, to serve the Lord.**

**Glory to the Father, and to the Son,
and to the Holy Spirit;
as it was in the beginning, is now
and shall be for ever. Amen.**

SCRIPTURE
READING
Matthew 18.1–5, 10

At that time the disciples came to Jesus and asked,
'Who is the greatest in the kingdom of heaven?' He
called a child, whom he put among them, and said,
'Truly I tell you, unless you change and become like
children, you will never enter the kingdom of heaven.
Whoever becomes humble like this child is the greatest
in the kingdom of heaven. Whoever welcomes one such
child in my name welcomes me. Take care that you do
not despise one of these little ones; for, I tell you, in
heaven their angels continually see the face of my
Father in heaven.'

REFLECTION

Eyes look out from this hand, watching us as we watch
them. Watching can sometimes have a passive, almost
negative connotation, the cool detached observer, or
the voyeur who watches for private pleasure, the arm-
chair critic who looks for faults, only to criticize. But
there is a divine strand to watching that is far from
passive, detached or critical.

This hand speaks to me of a passionate intensity of
watching, the sort of watching you do at a bedside as
someone slips away into death. My brother and I sat
beside my mother as she died; ceaselessly watching,
alert for any change, a vigil accompanied by the nurse
who shared my intensity. She said at one point, 'It only
hurts because you love.' So this watching is an involved
watching, a watching with all our heart and soul – the
gaze of love.

Matthew speaks of our guardian angel whose task it
is to look two ways, to watch over us and to gaze on
the face of God. An angel who makes that connection
between us and God, who holds that gaze towards God
even when our distracted attention darts here and
there. This angel hand is part of that gaze, connecting
both sides of the coin, the human and the divine, the
loving and the hurting, and holding us in the tension of
that wholeness. And, somehow, as we are held in the

tension of that wholeness, it allows us to face our true selves, to gaze upon ourselves with the gaze of love.

MUSIC *A time of meditation*

SILENCE We take into the silence those who have watched over us, and those we watch over.

INVOCATION TO THE WATCHERS
You watchers who ceaselessly gaze
on the face of God's glory,
you who perceive the love and the agony,
the brilliance and the shadow it casts:
help us now to attend to that same mystery.
You hold us in the gaze of love,
passionate intensity,
understanding all,
forgiving all,
redeeming the depths of our darkness.

PRAYERS OF RECOGNITION
We bring to God all that diverts our attention, our busyness and preoccupation, and we let it go.

Cantor: Understanding all, forgiving all
All: Redeem the depths of our darkness

We bring to God the surface image that we present to the outside world, and where it is untrue, we let it go.

Cantor: Understanding all, forgiving all
All: Redeem the depths of our darkness

We bring to God all that we seek to hide, all that we are ashamed of, and we let it go.

Cantor: Understanding all, forgiving all
All: Redeem the depths of our darkness

And because we are held in the gaze of love, we
dare to believe that we are loved and loveable, and
we offer ourselves.

Cantor: With your passionate intensity
All: Hold us in the gaze of love

We bring to God our true, inner self, longing to find
expression, and we offer it.

Cantor: With your passionate intensity
All: Hold us in the gaze of love

We bring to God our freedom, our ability, our gifted-
ness, and we offer it.

Cantor: With your passionate intensity
All: Hold us in the gaze of love

PRAYERS OF *A time of open prayer when we can bring to God*
INTERCESSION *people and situations that we care about*

After each intercession
Let us pray to the Lord
Lord have mercy

CLOSING PRAYER   **O God,**
open our eyes,
bridge the chasm of our imagination;
pierce us with your stare,
penetrate our defences,
face us with ourselves,
that we might behold your face,
see as we are seen
and know as we are known
even though the glass be dark.
Amen.

RAPHAEL

– the call to touch

Entertaining angels unawares, recognizing the touch of God

OPENING PRAYER

O God who heals,
circle our hearts,
centre our minds,
still our bodies,
be present to us now.
Amen.

CANTICLE
A Song of St Anselm,
Archbishop of
Canterbury, who died
in 1109

Jesus, like a mother you gather your people to you;
you are gentle with us as a mother with her children.

**Often you weep over our sins and our pride,
tenderly you draw us from hatred and judgement.**

You comfort us in sorrow and bind up our wounds,
in sickness you nurse us, and with pure milk you
feed us.

**Jesus, by your dying we are born to new life;
by your anguish and labour we come forth in joy.**

Despair turns to hope through your sweet goodness;
through your gentleness we find comfort in fear.

**Your warmth gives life to the dead,
your touch makes sinners righteous.**

Lord Jesus, in your mercy heal us;
in your love and tenderness remake us.

**In your compassion bring grace and forgiveness,
for the beauty of heaven may your love prepare us.**

**Glory to the Father, and to the Son,
and to the Holy Spirit;
as it was in the beginning, is now
and shall be for ever. Amen.**

SCRIPTURE
READING
1 Kings 19.4–9

But Elijah himself went a day's journey into the wilderness, and came and sat down under a solitary broom tree. He asked that he might die: 'It is enough; now, O LORD, take away my life, for I am no better than my ancestors.' Then he lay down under the broom tree and fell asleep. Suddenly an angel touched him and said to him, 'Get up and eat.' He looked, and there at his head was a cake baked on hot stones, and a jar of water. He ate and drank, and lay down again. The angel of the LORD came a second time, touched him, and said, 'Get up and eat, otherwise the journey will be too much for you.' He got up, and ate and drank; then he went in the strength of that food for forty days and forty nights to Horeb the mount of God. At that place he came to a cave, and spent the night there.

REFLECTION

This angel hand tells of God's reaching down to us. It tells of a God who wants to inspire and energize us. This downward curving finger comes at life from an oblique angle, it suggests a less than straightforward connection. It's a playful finger, almost tickling us into a response, provoking us to reach up and touch it, to connect, to play.

Raphael walked alongside his companions as a stranger on the road, joining them on their journey. Angels are often entertained unawares! But somehow, in the encounter, he brings encouragement, new energy, new hope, he heals and animates. The name Raphael means 'God has healed'.

On the road to Emmaus the disciples are dejected and despairing; they meet a stranger whom they finally come to recognize in the breaking of bread. The encounter gives new hope, new energy, new direction.

In this hand, a delicate touch, a glancing encounter, a chance connection is all that is needed for the electricity to flow, for the energy to be shared. It provokes us to stretch beyond the familiar, to reach out of our comfort zone and to be surprised as we discover new places of nurturing and connection that enable us to go on growing and loving and giving.

MUSIC   *A time of meditation*

SILENCE   We think of the strangers we have encountered today or in our lives. Have we been entertaining angels unawares?

INVOCATION TO
RAPHAEL   O Raphael, announcing 'God has healed', you whose touch connecting earth and heaven, empowers, inspires, and moves us. You who go unseen, unrecognized, mysterious companion, oblique animation, with power from on high: point us to the presence within, to the energy of Love.

PRAYERS OF
RECOGNITION   We bring to God all that is disheartened, discouraged and exhausted in us, and we let it go.

Cantor: Lord Jesus, in your mercy heal us
All: **In your love and tenderness remake us**

We bring to God all that is cynical, hardened and resigned in us, and we let it go.

Cantor: Lord Jesus, in your mercy heal us
All: In your love and tenderness remake us

We bring to God all that is stale, flat and lifeless in us, and we let it go.

Cantor: Lord Jesus, in your mercy heal us
All: In your love and tenderness remake us

And because we believe that God does heal us, we bring to God all that nourishes us, all that inspires us, and we offer it.

Cantor: Rouse us to walk again
All: Nourish us with the bread of mystery

We bring to God all that is innocent in us, all that is childlike and hopeful in us, and we offer it.

Cantor: Rouse us to walk again
All: Nourish us with the bread of mystery

We bring to God all that is fresh, all that is animated and alive in us, and we offer it.

Cantor: Rouse us to walk again
All: Nourish us with the bread of mystery

PRAYERS OF
INTERCESSION
A time of open prayer when we can bring to God people and situations that we care about

After each intercession
Let us pray to the Lord
Lord have mercy

CLOSING PRAYER
**Healing God,
reach out to touch us in our weakness,
rouse us to walk again,
and nourish us with the bread of mystery, that,
without easy answers,
without cheap grace,
we may bear witness
to your transforming energy in us.
Amen.**

SERAPH

– the call to speak

*Overcoming feelings of
inadequacy, recognizing our
own calling*

OPENING PRAYER   O God who calls us to reach out,
circle our hearts,
centre our minds,
still our bodies,
be present to us now.
Amen.

CANTICLE   Let my cry come before you, O Lord;
Psalm 119.169–173   give me understanding, according to your word.

**Let my supplication come before you;
deliver me, according to your promise.**

My lips shall pour forth your praise,
when you have taught me your statutes.

**My tongue shall sing of your word,
for all your commandments are righteous.**

Let your hand reach out to help me,
for I have chosen your commandments.

**Glory to the Father, and to the Son,
and to the Holy Spirit;
as it was in the beginning, is now
and shall be for ever. Amen.**

SCRIPTURE
READING
Isaiah 6.5–7

And I said: 'Woe is me! I am lost, for I am a man of unclean lips, and I live among a people of unclean lips; yet my eyes have seen the King, the LORD of hosts!' Then one of the seraphs flew to me, holding a live coal that had been taken from the altar with a pair of tongs. The seraph touched my mouth with it and said: 'Now that this has touched your lips, your guilt has departed and your sin is blotted out.'

REFLECTION

I love the narrow elongated fingers of this hand, the fragility, the pale other-worldliness reaching out to us. For me the eye became a burning coal, leaving a gash of a wound that breaks open this delicate hand, like the wounds of crucifixion. This is a powerful image, but its power comes from its fragility.

So often, when we reach out to others it is from a position of power. We like to be able to help people, solve their problems, to make a difference, to be capable, to be good at what we do, to be able. But this very strength and capability is what distances us. Like the people in suits who turn up in regeneration areas, we can become part of the problem.
To be able to reach out, Isaiah, like so many of the prophets, had to accept that it was his very woundedness, his weakness, that God would use to connect with people. If we want to make a difference, we must dare to reach out from our inadequacy, our own brokenness. It's a costly way. We must risk being hurt. We must allow the fire to get into our bloodstream and sear through our veins with unstoppable life.

MUSIC

A time of meditation

SILENCE

We take into the silence the weaknesses and vulnerabilities that we recognize in ourselves, and those to whom we are called to reach out.

INVOCATION TO
THE SERAPHS

O Seraphs, you burning ones,
you who carry the living flame
from the heart of God,
enduring the costly burden;
your hand reaches out
to make the stigmatic connection:
burn through
our coldness,
preoccupation
and indifference
with your healing woundedness.

PRAYERS OF
RECOGNITION

We bring to God all that is fearful in us, all that
paralyses and prevents us, and we let it go.

Cantor: Burn through our coldness
All: With your healing woundedness

We bring to God all that is indifferent, all that is hardened and unmoved in us, and we let it go.

Cantor: Burn through our coldness
All: With your healing woundedness

We bring to God all that crowds out our care, our
busyness and preoccupation, and we let it go.

Cantor: Burn through our coldness
All: With your healing woundedness

And because we *are* connected through God, we
bring to God all that moves us, our compassion and
understanding, and we offer it.

Cantor: Give us hands that reach and lips that
            speak
All: Alive with your life

We bring to God our courage, our strength and our determination, and we offer it.

Cantor: Give us hands that reach and lips that speak
All: Alive with your life

We bring to God our freedom, our ability, our gifted-ness, and we offer it.

Cantor: Give us hands that reach and lips that speak
All: Alive with your life

PRAYERS OF INTERCESSION   *A time of open prayer when we can bring to God people and situations that we care about*

After each intercession
Let us pray to the Lord
Lord have mercy

CLOSING PRAYER   **O God,
ignite our lips with that same passion
burning in your heart of love,
that we might be the hands that reach,
the lips that speak,
the *Angelos*
alive with your life,
messengers of divine empowerment.
Amen.**

SANCTUS

– the call to worship

*Open questions, open horizons
and unresolved chords in
the music of heaven*

OPENING PRAYER O God who calls us to silence,
circle our hearts,
centre our minds,
still our bodies,
be present to us now.
Amen.

CANTICLE On God alone my soul in stillness waits;
Psalm 62.1–2, 5–8 from him comes my salvation.

**He alone is my rock and my salvation,
my stronghold, so that I shall never be shaken.**

Wait on God alone in stillness, O my soul;
for in him is my hope.

**He alone is my rock and my salvation,
my stronghold, so that I shall not be shaken.**

In God is my strength and my glory;
God is my strong rock; in him is my refuge.

**Put your trust in him always, my people;
pour out your hearts before him, for God is our
refuge.**

**Glory to the Father, and to the Son,
and to the Holy Spirit;
as it was in the beginning, is now
and shall be for ever. Amen.**

SCRIPTURE
READING
Revelation 8.1–4

When the Lamb opened the seventh seal, there was silence in heaven for about half an hour. And I saw the seven angels who stand before God, and seven trumpets were given to them. Another angel with a golden censer came and stood at the altar; he was given a great quantity of incense to offer with the prayers of all the saints on the golden altar that is before the throne. And the smoke of the incense, with the prayers of the saints, rose before God from the hand of the angel.

REFLECTION

I find this perhaps the most 'quirky' of the angel hands. To me it is like an orchestral conductor holding a moment in a piece of music. It is an image full of tension and promise, full of questions – a crossroads, with a choice of paths forwards. The provocative curve of the finger suggests a different way of approach. Instead of straight-line logic, it allows for less certainty and more imagination.

R. S. Thomas talks about a fast God, always leaving just as we arrive, always just out of reach, beckoning us on to a further horizon. Whenever we feel we have arrived, in our understanding, in our prayer, in our living, God is always one step ahead of us, just over the horizon. But that's not the kind of God people want: we want certainty, a changeless comfortable God, we want answers. But if we are living authentically, life keeps asking more questions.

If we can dare to let go of the certainties, if we can hold back from formulaic answers, if we can resist the desire to resolve all of the tensions and allow the questions time to be with us, if we can love the questions, we may find ourselves caught up in the heavenly Sanctus and the moment of silence.

MUSIC   *A time of meditation*

SILENCE   We share in the silence of heaven, and so connect earth and heaven in ourselves.

INVOCATION TO
THOSE ANGELS
CRYING SANCTUS

O you who sing before God's throne,
whose voices repeat in heavenly chorus
the eternal Sanctus,
you whose finger holds the moment of suspense,
the hanging, unresolved cadence,
the uncomfortable moment of silence,
you whose finger holds the question
that is leading us beyond ourselves:
provoke imagination
to stretch our wordy liturgies and rigid doctrines,
to go beyond our comprehension,
just over our horizon.

PRAYERS OF
RECOGNITION

We bring to God all that distorts us, the unhealthy tensions, all that is out of balance in our lives, and we let it go.

Cantor: Wait on God alone in stillness, O my soul
All: For in him is my hope

We bring to God all of our busyness, where we are over-stretched, over-committed, over-wound, and we let it go.

Cantor: Wait on God alone in stillness, O my soul
All: For in him is my hope

We bring to God all that diminishes us, that stifles our imagination and limits our horizon, and we let it go.

Cantor: Wait on God alone in stillness, O my soul
All: For in him is my hope

And because we are surrounded by so great a cloud
of witnesses, we bring to God all that prompts us to
be creative, that provokes us to be imaginative, and
we offer it.

Cantor: Pour out your hearts before him
All: For God is our refuge

We bring to God the experiences that stretch us, that
beckon us towards new horizons, and we offer them.

Cantor: Pour out your hearts before him
All: For God is our refuge

We bring to God our unresolved questions and our
hunger for maturity, and we offer it.

Cantor: Pour out your hearts before him
All: For God is our refuge

PRAYERS OF   *A time of open prayer when we can bring to God*
INTERCESSION   *people and situations that we care about*

After each intercession
Let us pray to the Lord
Lord have mercy

CLOSING PRAYER   **Holy God,**
connect us with the heartbeat of your music,
touch us with the silence of your presence.
Call us out from where we are comfortable
to find you
in the tensions and the questions.
Amen.

GABRIEL

– the call to sanctified
ordinariness

*The incarnation, the Word
made flesh in us, shows us
heaven in ordinary*

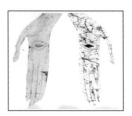

OPENING PRAYER O God who shows us incarnation,
circle our hearts,
centre our minds,
still our bodies,
be present to us now.
Amen.

CANTICLE My soul proclaims the greatness of the Lord,
Magnificat my spirit rejoices in God my Saviour;
he has looked with favour on his lowly servant.

**From this day all generations will call me blessed;
the Almighty has done great things for me
and holy is his name.**

He has mercy on those who fear him,
from generation to generation.

**He has shown strength with his arm
and has scattered the proud in their conceit,**

Casting down the mighty from their thrones
and lifting up the lowly.

**He has filled the hungry with good things
and sent the rich away empty.**

**Glory to the Father, and to the Son,
and to the Holy Spirit;
as it was in the beginning, is now
and shall be for ever. Amen.**

SCRIPTURE
READING
Luke 1.26–28, 35

In the sixth month the angel Gabriel was sent by God to a town in Galilee called Nazareth, to a virgin engaged to a man whose name was Joseph, of the house of David. The virgin's name was Mary. And he came to her and said, 'Greetings, favoured one! The Lord is with you.' The angel said to her, 'The Holy Spirit will come upon you, and the power of the Most High will overshadow you; therefore the child to be born will be holy; he will be called Son of God.'

REFLECTION

These two hands, mirroring one another, hold together for me the divinity and the humanity. At first sight, the gold hand seems ethereal and heavenly, while the black-and-white hand seems like an ordnance survey map with the paths and hills of an earthed landscape. But the two hands mirror one another and belong to one another as part of one body. And so they challenge our separation of sacred and secular, body and spirit. They bring us to a deeper holding together, a deeper sense of integration.

These hands seem to convey something of this holding together, the divine and the human. Here is a deeply materialistic faith, taking seriously the physical world, matter, flesh, shot through with Spirit. We have 'treasure in clay pots', the Word made flesh, the incarnation that Gabriel announced to Mary. And that holding together is not just in Jesus, but in each one of us.

These hands are open as an invitation to co-operate with God, a vocation to sanctified ordinariness, a vocation to be truly and fully ourselves. Our vocation is to be 'truly madly deeply' ourselves for God. As we become more authentically ourselves, we allow the Word to become flesh in us. The gold shines through and we live as people of the incarnation in the everyday.

MUSIC   *A time of meditation*

SILENCE   We reflect on some of the ordinary tasks and encounters in the Monday to Saturday parts of our lives, and how God comes to us to sanctify the ordinary.

INVOCATION TO   O Gabriel, herald of the incarnation,
GABRIEL   you who overshadow us with fearful greeting:
announce the Word made flesh in us,
treasure in our clay.
You who map the paths,
the plains and contours of our lives,
with your protecting symmetry:
reveal in us our calling,
discern in us vocation,
sanctified ordinariness,
divine image in the everyday.

PRAYERS OF   We bring to God our divided selves, our Sunday
RECOGNITION   best and the Monday to Saturday rest, all that we
separate into sacred and secular, and we let the
false divisions go.

Cantor: Alpha and Omega, beginning and end
All: **In all and through all, you are God**

We bring to God our divided lives, successes and failures, pride and shame, and we let the false divisions go.

Cantor: Alpha and Omega, beginning and end
All: **In all and through all, you are God**

We bring to God our divided hearts, loves and hates, prejudices and projections, and we let the false divisions go.

Cantor: Alpha and Omega, beginning and end
All: In all and through all, you are God

And because we have treasure in clay jars, we bring
to God our body, all that we touch and taste, and we
offer it.

Cantor: You are the Word made flesh
All: Word become flesh in us

We bring to God our mind, all that we think and
imagine, and we offer it.

Cantor: You are the Word made flesh
All: Word become flesh in us

We bring to God our spirit, all that is unique in us,
and we offer it.

Cantor: You are the Word made flesh
All: Word become flesh in us

PRAYERS OF   *A time of open prayer when we can bring to God*
INTERCESSION   *people and situations that we care about*

After each intercession
Let us pray to the Lord
Lord have mercy

CLOSING PRAYER   **O God our potter,**
see us as we might be.
Form in us your purpose,
shape in us your features,
that within the freedom of your love
we may find the space to be ourselves,
mirroring your image,
following your Way.
Amen.

EPIPHANY
Strangers and Pilgrims

Magi Hands
Discerning Our Giftedness

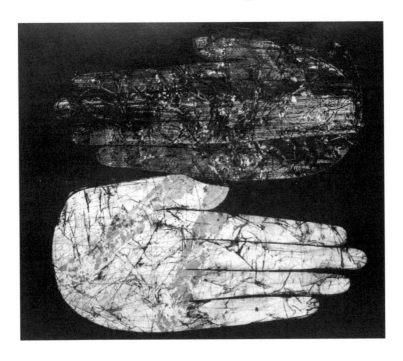

INTRODUCTION

Jake and I were invited to create an installation at the Greenbelt Festival in 2005, an exhibition of his images, combined with a workshop where people could explore their own hands in deepening spirituality. The distinctive hand shape of the Magi hands is based on that of a Native American image and seems to express the strangeness of the Magi, a very different culture coming in from outside. Two years later three of these same images returned to Greenbelt in a project we called 'Centre and Circumference'. Now enlarged to huge proportions they formed three sides of a worship space where we encouraged people to be still within all the hustle and bustle of the festival.

These liturgies were crafted to give shape to the space, and, using the haunting music of John Tavener's 'Prayer of the Heart', many were drawn to a profound stillness. The images and liturgies have been used in many different settings, in churches, cathedrals, retreat houses and arts centres, to explore the gift of God's calling. It has also been interesting to hear how people of different faiths have responded to these images. They have been found to be open enough for people of different faiths to encounter them in their own way.

In Matthew's account of the Christmas story (Matthew 2.1–12), the Christ Child is visited by the Magi, philosophers from the East, astrologers who have seen the sign of this new birth in the heavens. Western Christianity has popularized the Magi as three kings or wise men, though their number has only been inferred from the three gifts they brought, gold, frankincense and myrrh. In a world so divided into Jews and Gentiles, the children of God and the others, it is surprising that these witnesses were not Jews but Zoroastrians from Persia. This birth is destined from the beginning to break down barriers, to touch the whole world.

The Magi travel to the capital city, to the palace of King Herod in search of the one 'who has been born king of the Jews', but find the child in a very different setting, in a humble family. Herod seeks to trap them into betraying Jesus, but they are warned in a dream and return by another road.

This early example of different faith traditions coming together has led to an exploration of our differences. What do we bring to one another when we meet across the divides of religion and culture? What can we discover when science and religion meet? Who are we when we dig down into our own subconscious, when we move through different stages in our lives?

The weeks after Christmas, and the festival of the Epiphany, give a focus for this exploration. There are six Magi, six very different gifts for us to discover.

Gift Bearer recalls the Magi bringing their gifts to the Child; it explores our charism or 'calling-gift'; it is about us needing to empty our hands to receive the needful gifts of grace that God gives us to match our vocation, whatever that is to be.
Interpreter speaks particularly to the meeting of different cultures and faiths, and the need for mutual respect in that encounter, based on a common humanity and our equal value as children of God.
Exile is about what it means to move out of our comfort zone, to leave behind the familiar landmarks, to willingly embrace the wilderness. It looks at the wisdom of the street, hard won through experience, so needed in our poorest communities.

Dreamer remembers how the Magi were warned in a dream to go home by another road. It explores the world of our unconscious mind, the prompting of our conscience, the world of our deepest drives and desires. It encourages us to dream God's dream of a very different world of justice and peace.

Astrologer offers us the gift of perspective, echoing images from the surface of the moons of Saturn; this star gazer brings together the insights of science, the questions of cosmology, to discern the hand of the maker in the fabric of creation.

Searcher brings us right down to earth through the archaeology of the spirit, digging down into our own life story to find the roots of our faith. This is a process of unlearning as we test, in the second half of life, all that we once thought true.

These Magi help us to appreciate our own giftedness, and to hear God's call to search for him beyond the horizon of our experience.

GIFT BEARER

– the gift of integrity

*Emptying our hands to receive
our unique charism, God's
calling-gift*

OPENING PRAYER   O God who reaches out to us,
circle our hearts,
centre our minds,
still our bodies,
be present to us now.
Amen.

CANTICLE   My heart is ready, O God, my heart is ready;
Psalm 108.1–6   I will sing and give you praise.

**Awake, my soul; awake, harp and lyre,
that I may awaken the dawn.**

I will give you thanks, O Lord, among the peoples;
I will sing praise to you among the nations.

**For your loving-kindness is as high as the heavens
and your faithfulness reaches to the clouds.**

Be exalted, O God, above the heavens
and your glory over all the earth.

**That your beloved may be delivered,
save us by your right hand and answer me.**

**Glory to the Father, and to the Son,
and to the Holy Spirit;
as it was in the beginning, is now
and shall be for ever. Amen.**

SCRIPTURE   On entering the house, they saw the child with Mary
READING   his mother; and they knelt down and paid him hom-
Matthew 2.11   age. Then, opening their treasure-chests, they of-
fered him gifts of gold, frankincense, and myrrh.

REFLECTION   The Magi brought gifts for the child, gifts of significance, declaring, showing forth, the meaning of this
birth.

In this broad hand we trace the distinctive imprint of
circled lines. The gold squares seem to be ordered,
they suggest a conscious proffering of gifts. Look,
here are my gifts laid out, the very best I have, finest
gold, yet paper thin. Will it be accepted, will it be
enough? Somehow I have always imagined the Magi
bringing very solid, weighty, valuable gifts, which
have felt out of place with the baby born in poverty,
in a stable. But perhaps these gifts were more mod-
est, thin fragments, the best that could be managed?

But the gift and the hand are one; the gold bears the
distinctive fingerprint of the giver. It is transparent;
you can see the giver through the gift. The Greek
word for gift shares the same root as that of calling –
charism – we are gifted according to our vocation.
We are given the needful gifts of grace to match our
calling, equipped to enable us to fulfil our task. All
things come from you and of your own do we give
you. Fruit of the womb and work of human love, we
shall become a living sacrifice. God does not want
our money, our things; God wants our selves, our
gifts freely offered. Our gifts are not separate, but
part of us, 'what can I give Him poor as I am? Give my
heart!'

I love the spots of gold at the fingertips, it suggests
continuity, integrity; this is not just a one-off action
of giving, it is a continuation of a life of generosity,
right to the fingertips. This same generosity extends

beyond the gift. The Magi are generous in their appre-
ciation, in their approach. They do not judge by outward appearance, but find the gold in the manger.

MUSIC   *A time of reflection*

SILENCE   We think of the gifts we have been given, however
fragile, and the charism with which we have been
called.

INVOCATION TO   O Gift Bearer,
THE MAGI   whose outstretched palm offers
treasures of meaning,
fragments of understanding,
tissue-thin oblation,
catching the reflected light
from newborn eyes:
may your homage
lift our own inadequacy,
the best we have to give
to acknowledge
Love's Epiphany.

Our hands are full, cluttered, compromised,
possessed by possession,
defined by acquisition;
our giving
rarely unconditional
rings hollow,
betrays our emptiness.

We long for your charism,
continuity of gift and giver,
more than skin deep,
integrity to your fingertips,

ability and vocation
met in that deep resonance
of divine generosity.

We bring to God all that we try to hold, all that fills
our hands, all that is not true gift, and we let it go.

Cantor: Kyrie, Kyrie, Eleison
All: **Kyrie, Kyrie, Eleison**

We bring to God all that is shallow, hollow and
empty, all that is not true gift, and we let it go.

Cantor: Christe, Christe, Eleison
All: **Christe, Christe, Eleison**

We bring to God all that we vainly strive to be, our
ambition and image, all that is not true gift, and we
let it go.

Cantor: Kyrie, Kyrie, Eleison
All: **Kyrie, Kyrie, Eleison**

And because we are loved, we bring to God all the
fragments of light in us, all that is true gift, and we
offer it.

Cantor: Gloria, Gloria, Gloria, in excelsis Deo
All: **Gloria, Gloria, Gloria, in excelsis Deo**

We bring to God all that is deep, true and connected
in us, all that is true gift, and we offer it.

Cantor: Gloria, Gloria, Gloria, in excelsis Deo
All: **Gloria, Gloria, Gloria, in excelsis Deo**

We bring to God our hopes and dreams and possibilities, all that is true gift, and we offer it.

Cantor: Gloria, Gloria, Gloria, in excelsis Deo
All: Gloria, Gloria, Gloria, in excelsis Deo

PRAYERS OF   *A time of open prayer when we can bring to God*
INTERCESSION   *people and situations that we care about*

After each intercession
Let us pray to the Lord
Lord have mercy

CLOSING PRAYER   **Gifting God,**
cut to the centre of our busy emptiness
that we may let go all our anxious creations
and with open, empty hands
receive your calling-gift;
hold us in your gaze of love
where we are seen and known as gift,
original blessing,
children of light.
Amen.

INTERPRETER

– the gift of wisdom

Finding common humanity and mutual respect in a multi-faith world

OPENING PRAYER   O God who comes to meet us,
circle our hearts,
centre our minds,
still our bodies,
be present to us now.
Amen.

CANTICLE   Wisdom cries out in the street;
Proverbs 1.20–24   in the squares she raises her voice.

**At the busiest corner she cries out;
at the entrance of the city gates she speaks:**

'How long, O simple ones, will you love being simple?
How long will scoffers delight in their scoffing
and fools hate knowledge?

**Give heed to my reproof; I will pour out my
thoughts to you;
I will make my words known to you.**

I have called and you refused,
have stretched out my hand and no one heeded.'

**Glory to the Father, and to the Son,
and to the Holy Spirit;
as it was in the beginning, is now
and shall be for ever. Amen.**

SCRIPTURE
READING
Matthew 2.1

In the time of King Herod, after Jesus was born in Bethlehem of Judea, Magi from the East came to Jerusalem.

REFLECTION

The Magi travelled from the East, emissaries of another faith, representatives of the Gentile nations come to acknowledge the birth of the Saviour.

These hands seem to signify something of this meeting of faiths and cultures, hands facing in different directions, like strangers meeting at the crossroads. Hands held out for comparison, common ground in a shared humanity, the gold glimmerings acknowledging the shared vocabulary of faith. These hands face one another, like a showing of wares, a weighing of value, the bartering of a marketplace. Insights and revelations arranged differently, but to the seeing eye, even here there is a deeper continuity.

Our own conversations in a multi-faith community require this same kind of meeting, and the learning of a common language of faith and values. We need interpreters who can do more than just translate the vocabulary, they need to be able to dwell in two worlds. Like Mandela in South Africa who realized he needed to learn Afrikaans if he was to begin to understand his oppressors. We need a proper sense of reserve in announcing our 'truth', a proper sense of respect in encountering another's 'truth', an acknowledgement that no one has a monopoly on God.

Meetings at the crossroads led to an exchange of knowledge and tradition, stories and sayings traded like silks. The wisdom tradition was woven from threads from Persia, Babylon, Arabia and Egypt, common property, an international possession.

The book of Proverbs reminds us that it is Sophia, Lady Wisdom, who stands at the crossroads; reason is making herself heard in the marketplace, offering knowledge rather than finest gold. Often it is the women in a divided community who make the first moves towards peace, who build the first bridges towards the incomer, who build networks of understanding across the playground.

We can recognize our own debate about the changing face of our communities as we incorporate other cultures and faiths. Some fear the differences, some appreciate the cross-fertilization as ideas and experience blend and mix. These Magi hands testify to the mutual enrichment that comes from diversity.

MUSIC *A time of reflection*

SILENCE We think of the people we meet who are very different to us, the crossroads encounters, those who have shared their depths with us.

INVOCATION TO O Interpreter,
THE MAGI you who stand at the crossroads of East and West,
exchanging silk and spice,
reason and philosophy,
moving between our different worlds,
learning our language, ways and moods:
open to us the treasures of your faith,
complement our experience with
Holy Wisdom.

Calm our fears at your strangeness,
make yourself heard
amidst the clamour of our certainties
to see beneath the surface of our differences
our common humanity,
longing and reaching beyond
our shared values and insights
marked in the print of our hands.

We meet you still
in the marketplace and corner shop,
at the crossroads of temple and church,
across the playground and workplace:
open our eyes to every encounter,
to reach out to meet your hand
in receiving and in giving,
in exchanging
Epiphany illumination.

PRAYERS OF
RECOGNITION

We bring to God our sense of our own rightness, our own certainties, and we lay them down.

Cantor: Kyrie, Kyrie, Eleison
All: Kyrie, Kyrie, Eleison

We bring to God our own fears of the stranger and of other ways of understanding, and we lay them down.

Cantor: Christe, Christe, Eleison
All: Christe, Christe, Eleison

We bring to God the barriers we erect in our own heart, that keep us apart, and we lay them down.

Cantor: Kyrie, Kyrie, Eleison
All: Kyrie, Kyrie, Eleison

And because we are all God's children, we bring to God our common humanity, and we offer it.

Cantor: Gloria, Gloria, Gloria, in excelsis Deo
All: Gloria, Gloria, Gloria, in excelsis Deo

We bring to God our mutual need, and we offer it.

Cantor: Gloria, Gloria, Gloria, in excelsis Deo
All: Gloria, Gloria, Gloria, in excelsis Deo

We bring to God the bridge we hope to build, and we offer it.

Cantor: Gloria, Gloria, Gloria, in excelsis Deo
All: Gloria, Gloria, Gloria, in excelsis Deo

PRAYERS OF   *A time of open prayer when we can bring to God*
INTERCESSION   *people and situations that we care about*

After each intercession
Let us pray to the Lord
Lord have mercy

CLOSING PRAYER   **Holy Spirit of God,
speak to us across the divides of language and culture,
overcome our prejudice and fear,
remind us that you are not to be owned or contained
but to be found in every human heart;
help us to follow you,
the Go-between God,
make us holy bridge-builders
at the crossroads of our communities.
Amen.**

EXILE

– the gift of discontent

*Strangers, migrants,
asylum seekers, building bridges
of wisdom*

OPENING PRAYER   O God for whom we reach,
circle our hearts,
centre our minds,
still our bodies,
be present to us now.
Amen.

CANTICLE   Happy are those who find wisdom,
Proverbs 3   and those who get understanding,

**For her income is better than silver,
and her revenue better than gold.**

She is more precious than jewels,
and nothing you desire can compare with her.

**Long life is in her right hand;
in her left hand are riches and honour.**

Her ways are ways of pleasantness,
and all her paths are peace.

**She is a tree of life to those who lay hold of her;
those who hold her fast are called happy.**

**Glory to the Father, to the Son,
and to the Holy Spirit;
as it was in the beginning, is now
and shall be for ever. Amen.**

SCRIPTURE   'And you, Bethlehem, in the land of Judah, are by
READING   no means least among the rulers of Judah; for from
Matthew 2.6 you shall come a ruler who is to shepherd my
             people Israel.'

REFLECTION   The Magi journeyed from the East. This hand bears
             the marks of hardship, dry, cracked skin, worn,
             scarred, evidence perhaps of a hard journey, a
             voluntary exile from home; a willing alienation as
             familiarity and comfort are left behind, all risked for
             this moment as earthy wisdom meets heavenly
             Word.

             This is not a conventional philosopher's hand, soft
             from the privilege of leisure, but a working hand,
             toughened, engaged and practical. Insights have
             come from hard graft, wisdom from experience
             tested in the fire. Like so many brought up on tough
             estates, in areas of deprivation, there is a deep wis-
             dom that defies, that survives. Who, 'going through
             the valley of dryness have found in it a well'. Wilder-
             ness cries out from this hand, a willing endurance of
             loss for the sake of truth. Exiled from Eden, now we
             have to sweat to scratch a living from the earth.

             This is the hand behind the proverbs, 'bottom-up'
             revelation, crossing cultures, recognized by the
             humble if shunned by the elite. Traders exiled to
             Egypt, to Babylon, to Persia, seeking the welfare of
             the city in which they found themselves. Like asylum
             seekers, immigrants in a strange land, exiles who
             have much to share, much to give.

MUSIC   *A time of reflection*

SILENCE   We think of the exile times for us, hard experiences
          that have shaped us, the nourishment we have
          found in the wilderness.

INVOCATION TO
THE MAGI

O Exile far from home,
an unfamiliar landscape shapes your hand,
cracked dry skin, calloused, hardened by necessity,
you willingly embrace this costly alienation,
sage of the street
straight-eyed plain talker,
your qualifications etched upon open palm
wrought through aching toil:
open to us your homespun proverbs,
market tales,
traditional remedies,
grass-roots revelation
of Holy Wisdom.
We look down on you at first,
we're more used to men in suits,
strings of letters after their name,
suitably spoken professionals;
we're wary of strangers,
especially foreigners,
suspicious of your dirty, workers' hands
and of our own.

Yet something in you draws us,
some echo of your exile
vibrates in harmony
with our own sense of loss of Eden's plenty,
provokes in us respect for weathered hardships,
a mutuality that leaves us heartened,
sensing the possibilities
in our own reach.

PRAYERS OF
RECOGNITION

We bring to God the people we look down on, the
simple, poor and homeless ones, we miss their
wisdom.

Cantor: Kyrie, Kyrie, Eleison
All: Kyrie, Kyrie, Eleison

We bring to God the cultures we exclude, religions, customs, traditions, we miss their wisdom.

Cantor: Christe, Christe, Eleison
All: Christe, Christe, Eleison

We bring to God the parts of ourselves that we undervalue, our feelings, doubts and weakness, we miss their wisdom.

Cantor: Kyrie, Kyrie, Eleison
All: Kyrie, Kyrie, Eleison

And because we are exiles, we bring to God our sense of belonging to another kingdom, and we offer it.

Cantor: Gloria, Gloria, Gloria, in excelsis Deo
All: Gloria, Gloria, Gloria, in excelsis Deo

We bring to God the wilderness that has brought us wisdom, and we offer it.

Cantor: Gloria, Gloria, Gloria, in excelsis Deo
All: Gloria, Gloria, Gloria, in excelsis Deo

We bring to God our longing for our own true home, and we offer it.

Cantor: Gloria, Gloria, Gloria, in excelsis Deo
All: Gloria, Gloria, Gloria, in excelsis Deo

PRAYERS OF   *A time of open prayer when we can bring to God*
INTERCESSION   *people and situations that we care about*

After each intercession
Let us pray to the Lord
Lord have mercy

CLOSING PRAYER

God of our Exile,
make us uncomfortable with easy answers,
discontented with shallow lives,
dissatisfied with empty promises;
awaken in us a longing for our true home,
alive, bright, sharp, full,
push us out of the deadly rut
and in the company of strangers
direct us on our journey home.
Amen.

DREAMER
– the gift of imagination

Listening to our
subconscious, taking another
road

OPENING PRAYER O God who speaks to our hearts,
circle our hearts,
centre our minds,
still our bodies,
be present to us now.
Amen.

CANTICLE When the Lord restored the fortunes of Zion,
Psalm 126.1–6 then were we like those who dream.

Then was our mouth filled with laughter
and our tongue with songs of joy.

Then said they among the nations,
'The Lord has done great things for them.'

The Lord has indeed done great things for us,
and therefore we rejoiced.

Restore again our fortunes, O Lord,
as the river beds of the desert.

Those who sow in tears
shall reap with songs of joy.

Glory to the Father, and to the Son,
and to the Holy Spirit;
as it was in the beginning, is now
and shall be for ever. Amen.

SCRIPTURE READING
Matthew 2.12

And having been warned in a dream not to return to Herod, they left for their own country by another road.

REFLECTION

The Magi were warned in a dream to return home by another road. Dreams are so important in the story of God's people, a potent means of communication, the interplay between the conscious and unconscious mind.

There are three hands in this image. In the foreground the clearest hand, perhaps can be for us the conscious mind, the world of actions and consequences. The palm is covered with lines like a map of hills and valleys; it has a solidity that anchors the whole picture. Behind it is the second hand, shadowy, less defined, perhaps the dream-like world of the unconscious? And between the two, a golden hand, echoes of the divine, meeting and interacting through our dreams and connecting across, from the troubled dream of the night, to the cold light of the morning? There are two fingers or paths, the different alternatives, a chance to return by another road?

Jung understood the search for God to be a search within, and described the depths of the unconscious mind, our parental archetypes and common memories. Reflecting on our dreams can help us to bring to the surface memories and concerns, influences and voices that may have been long buried.

Deprived of dream sleep we become unwell. Dreaming is an essential part of our living, central to the way we process experiences and lay down memories for the future. Problems and worries in our waking lives surface in our dreaming, and we need to be attentive to what is being processed in our subconscious. Sometimes dreams are jumbled and incoherent, at other times they are hard to distinguish from reality. Dreams can reveal to us possibilities and significance in otherwise mundane events. They can allow our imagination to play, to risk, to dare, in ways that would never be possible to our waking mind.

These hands may disturb or inspire us to reflect on our dreaming. They may lead us to think about the possibility of change, a different future, taking another road. They may inspire us to turn away from the road to Herod, to reject the distortions of power and privilege, and turn instead to another Way.

MUSIC   *A time of reflection*

SILENCE   We think of a dream that has disturbed or influenced us, we listen for our deepest intuitions, and for God speaking to our heart.

INVOCATION TO   O Dreamer,
DREAMER   you catch the starlit echoes of jumbled imagination,
memory's playfulness and Divine possibility;
shadowed night illuminates the morning,
lightens a path otherwise unseen.
Draw us past the solidity of today's events,
the fixedness of our expectations,
the memory of past hurts;
open us to the possibility of our dreaming,
waken us to such awareness,
disturb our complacency,
puncture overblown self-image,
release locked-in potential,
that we might know our selves
truly.

You disturb us from the nightmare
of distorted lives
where holy innocence is crushed by jackboot tread.

You open to us wells of creativity,
hidden depths of our own personality,
echoes of shared memory, parental voices,
and beneath it all
the hand of Life.

Sensing these alternatives
returning by another road
becomes our second nature.

PRAYERS OF   We bring to God the memories of past hurts pushed
RECOGNITION   down, repressed. Give us grace to encounter them
and let them go.

Cantor: Those who sow in tears
All: Shall reap with songs of joy

We bring to God any complacency, things we no
longer see, take for granted. Give us grace to
encounter them and let them go.

Cantor: Those who sow in tears
All: Shall reap with songs of joy

We bring to God our habits of conformity, the ruts in
which we tread, the patterns we repeat uncon-
sciously. Give us grace to encounter them and let
them go.

Cantor: Those who sow in tears
All: Shall reap with songs of joy

And because we are called to another road, we bring
to God the hidden depths of our own personality,
the deep wells of creativity in us, and we offer them.

Cantor: Then was our mouth filled with laughter
All: And our tongue with songs of joy

We bring to God our dreams of sword and
ploughshare peace, of vine and fig tree plenty, and
we offer them.

Cantor: Then was our mouth filled with laughter
All: And our tongue with songs of joy

We seek for courage in following imagination's star.
We bring to God the alternative patterns that we
might choose, the choices we have to make, and we
offer them.

Cantor: Then was our mouth filled with laughter
All: And our tongue with songs of joy

PRAYERS OF   *A time of open prayer when we can bring to God*
INTERCESSION   *people and situations that we care about*

After each intercession
Let us pray to the Lord
Lord have mercy

CLOSING PRAYER   **God of our deepest dream,**
your hand emboldens us
to dare, to risk, to change,
to follow imagination's star
into new possibilities and landscapes.
Dream in us your dream
of sword and ploughshare peace,
of vine and fig tree plenty,
that we might wake
to take another path.
Amen.

ASTROLOGER

– the gift of perspective

The questions of cosmology
meet the searchers for faith

OPENING PRAYER   O God who lightens our darkness,
circle our hearts,
centre our minds,
still our bodies,
be present to us now.
Amen.

CANTICLE   Bless the Lord all you works of the Lord:
Benedicite (selected   sing his praise and exalt him for ever.
verses from 1–6)

Bless the Lord you heavens:
sing his praise and exalt him for ever.

Bless the Lord you angels of the Lord:
bless the Lord all you his hosts;

Bless the Lord you waters above the heavens:
sing his praise and exalt him for ever.

Bless the Lord sun and moon:
bless the Lord you stars of heaven;

Bless the Lord light and darkness:
sing his praise and exalt him for ever.

Glory to the Father, and to the Son,
and to the Holy Spirit;
as it was in the beginning, is now
and shall be for ever. Amen.

SCRIPTURE
READING
Matthew 2.2

'Where is the child who has been born king of the Jews? For we observed his star at its rising, and have come to pay him homage.'

REFLECTION

The Magi were astrologers, they studied the stars, searching the sky for glimpses of meaning and significance. They believed that God revealed his purposes in the heavens. As 'Star-led Chieftains' they followed the star to discover the child in the manger who would be King of the Jews.

These hands are alight with stellar luminosity; this is reflected light, with an unearthly quality. It's like the surface of the moon, pockmarked with craters, impact points, oases of deep darkness. They speak of the immensity of creation, reminding us that we live in an obscure corner of just one galaxy among millions. These stargazers open to us the questions of cosmology, the interrelatedness of all creation. They stretch our understanding of God's purpose and activity in creation. The 'heavens are telling the glory of God'.

These hands help us to put our own concerns into perspective. They help us to lift up our eyes from the immediate day-to-day problems and worries of our lives, to wonder about what lies, in Micheal OSiadhail's words, 'beyond the beyond, beyond'. They hold part of the tension of God who made the universe, yet who knows our name, numbers the hairs on our head, watches every sparrow fall.

These astrologers' hands can help us as we wrestle with the insights of faith and science. These are the scientists of their day, gifted thinkers, whose patient observation, investigation and reflection bring them to the truth. These hands can help us not to be afraid of the insights of science, not to see science as a rival to our faith, but as a complementary discipline.

We are reminded that we are made of stardust. Like
Thomas the questioner, we are called to question
and test our faith in the fire of lived experience:
'I will not believe until I see the mark of the nails.'
Then we too will be able to say with conviction,
'My Lord and my God'.

MUSIC   *A time of reflection*

SILENCE   As we think of the night sky, the wonder of a
universe in such creative balance, we take into our
silence our own smallness in the face of such
immensity.

INVOCATION TO   O Astrologer,
ASTROLOGER   you who scan the immensity of creation,
searching for glimpses of meaning and purpose;
lift up our heads
in the darkness of a wakeful night,
raise our attention from the everyday routine
to seek with you
the one who lies beyond the furthest star
and within the nearest breath.

In your patient waiting, watching, wondering,
you discern the Maker's presence
reflected in a distant landscape,
the light of heaven
resting in a stable.

Give us courage to follow the star of our questioning,
investigate, penetrate,
see for ourselves the cratered mark of the nails,
daring to acknowledge doubt and uncertainty,
discovering faith that delights in exploration,
that in your reflected light
we may see Light.

PRAYERS OF
RECOGNITION

We bring to God the questions we have avoided, the challenges to our faith that we have met with unexamined certainties: we seek the light.

Cantor: The one who lies beyond the furthest star
All: And within the nearest breath

We bring to God our human formulations and doctrines, and where we have mistaken them for reality, we seek the light.

Cantor: The one who lies beyond the furthest star
All: And within the nearest breath

We bring to God the limitations of our horizon, our parochial preoccupations, our petty prejudices: we seek the light.

Cantor: The one who lies beyond the furthest star
All: And within the nearest breath

And because we are people of stardust, we wait, with open minds and hearts, for the next insight, the new discovery, the unfolding revelation: and we welcome your light.

Cantor: The light of heaven
All: Resting in a stable

We watch, with eyes on the horizon, waiting to see and know the truth for ourselves, for the mark of the nails: and we welcome your light.

Cantor: The light of heaven
All: Resting in a stable

We wonder, following the star of our questioning, explaining, testing, and finding your presence in the fire of our lived experience: and we welcome your light.

Cantor: The light of heaven
All: Resting in a stable

PRAYERS OF
INTERCESSION

*A time of open prayer when we can bring to God
people and situations that we care about*

After each intercession
Let us pray to the Lord
Lord have mercy.

CLOSING PRAYER

**God of the cosmos,
light of every star, motion of every atom,
immanent and transcendent,
expand our imagination by your immensity,
stretch our understanding,
bombard our false certainties,
break through the rigid surface of our doctrines
to find you with open heart and mind,
present in each one of us,
in every sparrow that falls.
Amen.**

SEARCHER

– the gift of unlearning

An archaeology of the spirit
in the second half of life

OPENING PRAYER O God who longs to be found by us,
circle our hearts,
centre our minds,
still our bodies,
be present to us now.
Amen.

CANTICLE
Psalm 63 O God, you are my God; eagerly I seek you;
my soul is athirst for you.

My flesh also faints for you,
as in a dry and thirsty land where there is no water.

So would I gaze upon you in your holy place,
that I might behold your power and your glory.

Your loving-kindness is better than life itself
and so my lips shall praise you.

I will bless you as long as I live
and lift up my hands in your name.

Glory to the Father, and to the Son,
and to the Holy Spirit;
as it was in the beginning, is now
and shall be for ever. Amen.

SCRIPTURE
READING
Matthew 2.8

'Go and search diligently for the child; and when you have found him, bring me word so that I may also go and pay him homage.'

REFLECTION

The Magi were searchers, seeking the newborn King. Their searching provoked Herod and the scribes to search their own traditions and scriptures.

The first thing that struck me in this hand were the lined circles in the palm; it's like a slice through a tree trunk, revealing the history of the tree, each ring a year of growth. In some softwood trees the rings would be wide and fleshy, indicating good conditions, speedy growth. In others there might be wide and narrow rings, showing the variations in the seasons and conditions. In a human life, the rapid growth and the uneven pattern might reflect a passing enthusiasm, or a coming and going in our relationship with God. Most of us will have known times when we have felt close to God, times of sap, and times where we have felt more distant, times of dryness. You can trace them like years of plenty and of poverty in the tree rings. But in this hand the pattern tells of a steady growth, there is a regularity that suggests this has been a disciplined and patient growing. There is a density of experience in this life, this hand has been steady, the breadth of the hand speaks of the years of steady hard-won growth. This is a strong hand, this wood will be hard, this life will weather the storms and challenges.

The layers of the tree rings also suggest an archaeology of the spiritual journey, a moving inwards, layer by layer, becoming aware of who we are, and what has shaped us. We expose each layer of ourselves to God, and allow God to reach us at a deeper level. Perhaps the dried blood-red patches in the image expose some of the pain of our life's journey, yet beneath it all the steady density continues. The exploration draws us inwards to our core, to the still centre of our being, and even in the space right at the heart, there we find God. Written into our very DNA, echoed in every person and every blade of grass, creation reveals the Creator.

The fingers of this hand are so long! They seem to be stretching out, searching for meaning, each like a path of light into the darkness. We look to so many externals to satisfy our yearning for God; even within the faith we search for motivational sermons, exciting worship, the latest course or retreat centre. We seek understanding in far places, we look far and wide for revelations and prophets and teachers, even for messiahs, and here it was all the time; in our own hand we find God, the Word made flesh in us, incarnation in the palm of our hand.

In the second half of our lives we often have to embrace a journey of unlearning. Those things that seemed so certain in our youth, the strengths that seemed so natural to us, the ambitions and drives that motivated us, all these can come to seem very limited, unsatisfying, partial. As we search for meaning and purpose in our lives, the hand of the Searcher may help us to become aware of our own inner archaeology, our own layers of experience. We may find ourselves arriving where we started, unlearning in order to learn anew.

MUSIC   *A time of reflection*

SILENCE   We reflect on our searching, for meaning and purpose, for happiness, for love, for faith, and on what we might need to unlearn.

INVOCATION TO
THE MAGI

O Searcher,
your broad hand tells of earthed wisdom;
no shallow enthusiasm, no ivory tower,
steady, persistent, faithful,
a density of experience,
years of patient waiting
to recognize the moment when it came:
kairos.

We who search now
follow the archaeology of your diligence,
the journeying outward, activity, enquiry, research,
courses, methods, gurus, latest news,
our first forays into the beyond,
only to come, as you came,
to find Life,
not out there, but here
in the still centre of our selves,
and in every other hand
creation's self-revelation
sacred to the core:
incarnate.

This unlearning has been a costly turning
from all that seemed so vital;
your hands bear the marks of painful transition,
raw blisters from the mattock and shovel
cutting the turf, down to find the 'natural';
your gift of healing Myrrh,
though stinging,
is welcome now.

PRAYERS OF
RECOGNITION

We bring to God all we hide in ourselves, all that we
are ashamed of and regret, and we let it go.

Cantor: Kyrie, Kyrie, Eleison
All: Kyrie, Kyrie, Eleison

We bring to God all the memories that we bury, all that has hurt us, and we let it go.

Cantor: Christe, Christe, Eleison
All: Christe, Christe, Eleison

We bring to God all that we have used for short-term satisfaction, and we let it go.

Cantor: Kyrie, Kyrie, Eleison
All: Kyrie, Kyrie, Eleison

And because God has sought us out and known us, we bring to God the layers of our own archaeology, the journey of self-discovery, and we offer it.

Cantor: Gloria, Gloria, Gloria, in excelsis Deo
All: Gloria, Gloria, Gloria, in excelsis Deo

We bring to God all that we are unlearning, all that we are letting go, for a new pattern to emerge, and we offer it.

Cantor: Gloria, Gloria, Gloria, in excelsis Deo
All: Gloria, Gloria, Gloria, in excelsis Deo

We bring to God all that is to be found in us, unrealized potential, unknown depths, and we offer it.

Cantor: Gloria, Gloria, Gloria, in excelsis Deo
All: Gloria, Gloria, Gloria, in excelsis Deo

PRAYERS OF   *A time of open prayer when we can bring to God*
INTERCESSION   *people and situations that we care about*

After each intercession
Let us pray to the Lord
Lord have mercy

CLOSING PRAYER

Searching God,
you meet us at every turn, in every moment,
smiling at our innocent certainty,
patient with our striving achievements,
longing to find and be found in us.
Hold us now in your steadiness,
that within the breadth of your strong hand
we may dare to empty our hands
and find you here.
Amen.

HOLY WEEK
Dying and Living

Christ Hands
Repairing Our Relationships

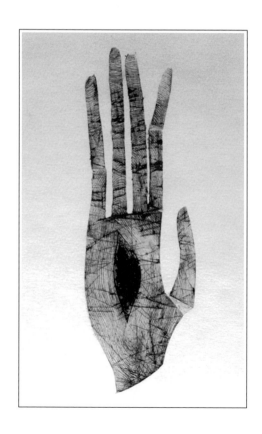

INTRODUCTION

These images were some of the earliest that Jake
Lever produced in this series of hands. They were
some of the first that fired my imagination, but some
of the hardest to read and interpret. After several
different approaches over a number of years they
began to speak into the agony of Holy Week. A traditional form for Good Friday meditation has been the
seven last words of Jesus from the cross. These
images began to provoke new insights into that
traditional framework, and I have bracketed them
with an image for the night of Maundy Thursday,
from the garden of Gethsemane, and an image from
the Empty Tomb, of resurrection.

I have used these in a number of different ways.
They can be used individually as a focus for worship
at the end of a Lent house group, and also in Holy
Week services as a focus for prayer and reflection.
They have also worked as a set on Good Friday to
provide the framework for reflection in a three-hour,
or last-hour service. Combined with silence and
pieces of music, the images provide a rich context
for reflection. This is the way that they have been set
out in this section, not as fully worked individual
liturgies, but as a series of reflections and prayers
designed to work as a whole.

Here is one suggestion of how this material could be
used for a service of one and a half hours on Good
Friday.

SERVICE PLANNING   The church or hall should be set out with a screen
and data projector to one side, but comfortably
visible to all. You may want to use a rough wooden
cross at the front as a focus for devotion in the

service. If you are using music with the images, you might like to consider extracts from James Macmillan's *Seven Last Words*, Karl Jenkins' *Requiem*, or Karl Jenkins' *Armed Man: A Mass for Peace.*

Good Friday Christ Hands – repairing our relationships

Hymn – Come and See (Graham Kendrick)

The service is divided into seven sections, each one consisting of an introduction to the image, a short extract of music, followed by a period of silence and then a final prayer.

1 **Father forgive** – transforming hurt and pain
The costly alternative at the heart of repairing relationships.

2 **My God, my God, why have you forsaken me?** – loss of faith and hope
Shouting at God when we are angry and hopeless.

Hymn – Heaven Shall Not Wait (John Bell and Graham Maule)

3 **Behold your son** – discerning interdependence
Creating new communities of care when others have been lost.

4 **I thirst** – our real needs
Acknowledging our own neediness, being able to receive from others.

Hymn – As the Deer (Martin Nystrom)

5 **Today you will be with me in paradise** – mending our brokenness
Unexpected generosity that brings out the best in us.

6 **It is finished** – honest endings
Recognizing death and what has been accomplished.

Hymn – Father I Place into Your Hands (Jenny Hewer)

7 **Into your hands I commend my spirit** – trusting in the darkness
Going on when it all seems hopeless.

Hymn – When I Survey (Isaac Watts)

The service may conclude with the reading of the end of the Passion Gospel, the account of Jesus' death on the cross. The people may come forward to pray at the foot of the cross, and then they leave the service in silence.

TAKE THIS CUP AWAY FROM ME

– our deepest feelings

*Daring to be real,
to own what is really
going on for us*

SCRIPTURE
READING
Luke 22.39–46 He came out and went, as was his custom, to the
Mount of Olives; and the disciples followed him.
When he reached the place, he said to them, 'Pray
that you may not come into the time of trial.' Then
he withdrew from them about a stone's throw, knelt
down, and prayed, 'Father, if you are willing, remove
this cup from me; yet, not my will but yours be
done.' Then an angel from heaven appeared to him
and gave him strength. In his anguish he prayed
more earnestly, and his sweat became like great
drops of blood falling down on the ground. When he
got up from prayer, he came to the disciples and
found them sleeping because of grief, and he said to
them, 'Why are you sleeping? Get up and pray that
you may not come into the time of trial.'

REFLECTION There is a drab greyness to this picture, it is colour-
less, washed out, and it evokes the dimness of night
in the garden of Gethsemane. Jesus is alone and
lonely, *'Could you not watch with me one brief hour?'*

There are shadows in the darker background, forces
at work, blurred images, much to be afraid of,
terrors half seen, all the more fearful. I wonder what
is in that darkness for us. What are we afraid of?
The dotted lines on the fingers suggest a direction
that has been mapped out, an inevitable path, a path
deliberately taken, one step at a time. *'Can this cup*

pass away from me?' Perhaps this is one more moment of choice, one path leads away, the others lead on. In the centre of the hand is a mass of darkness, 'a handful of dust'. Is this all my life has been, abandonment, misunderstanding, betrayal?

Sometimes at retirement or in mid life we come to look back at our life's work, and feel a sense of disappointment. Careers that have taken most of our energy and that seemed so important at the time, now seem pointless. Parents, when the children have left home, can feel the same sense of loss and disillusionment. We are left with a handful of dust.

In Gethsemane Jesus dared to own his deepest feelings, to voice his deepest longing, not to go through the coming trauma and pain and death. The same words are repeated in some form whenever a person is diagnosed with cancer or HIV or some other untreatable illness. 'Take this cup away from me.' At this terrible moment we long for reality to be different, for the miracle, for the respite, the powerful cure. It can be hard to own up to our real feelings, particularly for people of faith; we are expected to have spiritual resources to cope!

Perhaps this hand can give us permission to follow Jesus' example? Can we be equally honest and real about our feelings, and not have to pretend to be more able or competent than we are, not to be braver, holier, better than we really are? Can we dare to voice our own fears and feelings and doubts?

When we encounter people who seem to be 'too good to be true', it is often because they are! The real hero is not the one who feels no fear, but the one who knows the fear and goes on anyway.

In relationship we long for problems to be taken away from us, we sometimes choose to walk away

from situations or responsibilities rather than to
face up to them. Some will go through a series of
relationships repeating the same pattern of problems; they end up with a 'handful of dust' each time.
If we can dare to stick with it, to go through the
valley of the shadow of death, we will eventually
encounter the dawn.

SILENCE   Let's take into this time of reflection our own Gethsemane moments, our own fears and disappoint-
ments, and allow Jesus' honest hand to hold them.

MUSIC   *A time of meditation*

FINAL PRAYER   **Lord Jesus,**
we wait with you in the darkness;
we will watch with you
now in this moment when you need us.
Help us to learn from your honesty,
own our real feelings.
We don't want this cup.
Why me?
Give us grace to walk through the valley,
death's shadow,
hand full of dust,
and come to the dawn of a new day
with you.
Amen.

Concluding with

Into your hands, O Lord, I commend my spirit
For you have redeemed me, O Lord God of truth.

FATHER FORGIVE

– transforming hurt and pain

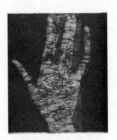

*The costly alternative
at the heart of repairing
relationships*

SCRIPTURE
READING
Luke 23.32–35 Two others also, who were criminals, were led away
to be put to death with him. When they came to the
place that is called The Skull, they crucified Jesus
there with the criminals, one on his right and one on
his left. Then Jesus said, *'Father, forgive them; for
they do not know what they are doing.'* And they cast
lots to divide his clothing. And the people stood by,
watching; but the leaders scoffed at him, saying, 'He
saved others; let him save himself if he is the Messiah
of God, his chosen one!'

REFLECTION The first words that Jesus speaks from the cross are
words of forgiveness. 'Father forgive them, they do
not know what they are doing.' These are words of
forgiveness even to those who have beaten and
mocked him, even to those who have nailed his
hands to the cross. Where all our human instincts
would be to curse and condemn, and to cry for
vengeance, for retribution, Jesus finds it in his heart
to forgive them.

The problem with our human instincts is that when
we have been hurt we want to hurt back. 'An eye for
an eye, a tooth for a tooth', a cycle of revenge which,
as Gandhi said, leaves the whole world blind.

This hand is raised as if in blessing. The texture is
complex, it bears the mark of laceration, scourging,

the blessing comes out of the heart of the suffering.
You can see an ascending gold strip rising through
the image, an indication of the divine presence, the
relationship between earth and heaven. It repre-
sents for us the central mystery of the cross – how
can something so cruel and deadly be transformed
into a blessing?

Jesus had said we should turn the other cheek, not
retaliate, that we should forgive as we have been
forgiven, seventy times seven. And here he has to
live out those words.

This is no cheap grace, these are no easy words, but
at the heart of the cross is the costly alternative, to
absorb and transform the hurts we receive, refusing
to let their poison continue to distort our relationships.

What do we do when we have been hurt or are in
pain, are we frozen in fear? Bullies seek the victim
who cannot move, paralysis seems to draw yet more
violence, to a continuing cycle of abuse. Or are we
hot with anger, wanting vengeance, to strike back?
Retribution leads to yet more violence, to a feud
over generations as we have seen in Northern
Ireland or in Palestine. Hot or cold, all roads seem
to lead to yet more hurting. Where do we go from
here?

There is movement in this hand, and to those in pain,
movement can bring relief, and even hope. Jesus
broke through the cycle of hurt and violence in a
radically new way. He endured the very worst and
gave the very best. He took the thorns, the mockery,
the scourge, the nails and spear, and absorbed it,
without striking back, and most importantly, he
asked God to forgive his tormentors.

This is the movement of the atonement, not a
sacrifice, but a willing forgiveness, a refusal to allow

violence to breed violence, and instead, to absorb
its hurt. In this way Jesus began to repair the relationships that had been so fractured. He was able
to forgive Peter for his denial, and Thomas for his
disbelief. I think even Judas' betrayal was included
in that forgiveness. And in redeeming those
relationships, so God was able to use the forgiveness
of Jesus to repair the broken relationship with
humanity as a whole.

SILENCE   Let's take into this time of reflection some of the
people and situations that have hurt us deeply, and
perhaps the times that we have wanted to hurt back.
And allow Jesus' hand of blessing to hold them.

MUSIC   *A time of meditation*

FINAL PRAYER   **Lord Jesus,**
at the heart of your cross
we find the costly alternative
to human cries for retribution and revenge.
You embrace the very worst we can throw at you,
absorbing its pain,
transforming its poison,
returning love for hate,
forgiving and redeeming us.
Give us that same grace to forgive,
repair our relationships,
open our hearts to love again.
Amen.

Concluding with

Into your hands, O Lord, I commend my spirit
For you have redeemed me, O Lord God of truth.

FORSAKEN

– loss of faith and hope

Shouting at God when we are angry and hopeless

SCRIPTURE READING
Matthew 27.41–46 'In the same way the chief priests also, along with the scribes and elders, were mocking him, saying, 'He saved others; he cannot save himself. He is the King of Israel; let him come down from the cross now, and we will believe in him. He trusts in God; let God deliver him now, if he wants to; for he said, "I am God's Son."' The bandits who were crucified with him also taunted him in the same way. From noon on, darkness came over the whole land until three in the afternoon. And about three o'clock Jesus cried with a loud voice, 'Eli, Eli, lema sabachthani?' that is, 'My God, my God, why have you forsaken me?'

REFLECTION This word from the cross is so very human, a feeling of having been forsaken, abandoned by God. 'My God, my God, why have you forsaken me?' In the garden Jesus had asked for this cup to pass away from him, he had hoped there could have been another way. But the soldiers came, the prayer seemed unanswered, and now the worst is happening and he feels that God has forsaken him.

This image is a very dark one; you have to strain to see the hand at all in the gloom. It echoes the darkness of Jesus' cry; it all feels lost and hopeless. In the palm is the nail, gold drips from the wound like blood, or like tears from an eye.

This image was created at the time of the tsunami in South East Asia and much of its darkness is rooted in the worldwide sense of desolation and shock that followed that event.

You have to let your eyes adjust to the darkness of this image, it slows you down, to stop and peer into its depths. Slowly some details emerge. There is the grey wood of the cross, the brown of the hand, our eyes are drawn to the wound, like a golden eye, drops of blood like tears flow from it in Jake Lever's familiar compression of wound/eye/glory imagery.

We are reminded of other times Jesus wept, over Jerusalem, over Lazarus; 'If you had been there' is the same accusation as 'Why have you forsaken me?' It's how we feel when our prayers seem to go unanswered, and God seems absent or distant. When the test results come back and we hear our worst fears confirmed, why me? When someone we love is hurt or dies, why, why them? Why couldn't you do something, what has my faith been for if you can't make any difference? Why have you forsaken me?

When we have those times when our faith is shaken, or when we feel angry with God, or abandoned by God, this cry of Jesus can give us permission to be totally honest with God, to express our anger, our hurt, our hopelessness, and to know that God hears us. That God weeps with us, that God's hands are sometimes tied by love, and that this cup cannot pass from us.

Jesus holds together the tension – 'my God' is such a strong, personal claim, 'why have you forsaken me' an equally strong sense of loss. It's an honesty that is familiar to the psalmist, but often lacking in the saccharine-sweet lyrics of some contemporary Christian songs. This image calls us to real honesty with God, and with ourselves, even to shout, even to be angry, to weep, to lose faith, confident that God can hold and contain our strongest feelings.

SILENCE   Take into this time of reflection some of the darker
times in our lives, times we have felt God has not
answered our prayers. And allow Jesus' hand of
honest questioning to hold them.

MUSIC   *A time of meditation*

FINAL PRAYER   **Gracious God,**
in the face of our desperate questioning
the desolation and abandonment we feel
when all our hopes have come to nothing,
all our dreams been dashed,
your tears bless us,
your fierce love penetrates the darkness,
accepting and containing our honest anger.
Hold us now as we cling to you
till the storm passes.
Amen.

Concluding with

Into your hands, O Lord, I commend my spirit
For you have redeemed me, O Lord God of truth.

BEHOLD
YOUR SON

– discerning interdependence

*Creating new communities
of care where others have been
lost*

SCRIPTURE
READING
John 19.25b–27

Meanwhile, standing near the cross of Jesus were his mother, and his mother's sister, Mary the wife of Clopas, and Mary Magdalene. When Jesus saw his mother and the disciple whom he loved standing beside her, he said to his mother, 'Woman, here is your son.' Then he said to the disciple, 'Here is your mother.' And from that hour the disciple took her into his own home.

REFLECTION

This word from the cross shows us Jesus' very human heart and his care for his mother and the beloved disciple, John. These two have come with him all the way, even to the foot of the cross, their grief has brought them together and Jesus asks them to care for one another when he is dead. *'Woman, behold your son, Son, behold your mother.'* In the face of his own death Jesus is creating new bonds of family and relationship, new levels of interdependence.

The image will speak differently to each of us. For some this will be the hand of a child in the hand of an adult, Mary and Jesus when he was young perhaps. For others this may speak of the child within each of us, the child that we once were, the vulnerable, trusting, innocent part of us. Even as adults, the loss of a parent can be painful and traumatic; for parents, the loss of a child can be even more so.

But in the centre of this tragic scene it is Jesus who is seeking to protect and care for his loved ones, to help them to know that they each have a purpose and a responsibility to each other after his death. It echoes his life's work, of bringing isolated and unloved people together into new communities of care. 'Look after my mum' is a very human response to an appalling situation.

These new relationships are not based upon ties of blood and family, but are creating a new family of choice. In a credit union we saw volunteers come together, many had disabilities, some were very lonely, yet each had so much to give. The common endeavour and strong sense of belonging was like a family, and was a basic building block for repairing communities. These hands echo the hands we raise to receive communion, there is an acknowledge-ment of a willingness to receive 'koinonia', the gift of relationship.

For Mary there will be so many memories, of an unlooked-for pregnancy, the stable, the manger, the boy growing up, lost in the Temple, their particular closeness, his tiny hand in hers for so many years. For Jesus and for each of us there is the inner child, the continuity of personality that stretches back to the beginning of each of our lives. For adults who have been abused as children, there is a special need to reconnect with this inner child who needs to find healing. For all of us there is a need to be connected with the child within if we are to enter the kingdom of heaven. We need to be able to play, to dance, to be foolish, to trust, and to cry.

SILENCE   Let's take into this time of reflection some of the people we rely on, those we can trust with our vulnerability, and those who rely on us, perhaps

from outside our family. And allow Jesus' hand of
new relationship to hold them.

SILENCE   *A time of meditation*

FINAL PRAYER   **Lord Jesus,**
you draw us into new patterns
of relationship and care;
you rebuild our broken communities
through your generous, inclusive love.
Connect us with the child within,
help us to trust and play,
to dance and cry
within the promise of your kingdom
where we shall see you face to face.
Amen.

Concluding with

Into your hands, O Lord, I commend my spirit
For you have redeemed me, O Lord God of truth.

I THIRST

– our real needs

Acknowledging our own
neediness, being able to
receive from others

SCRIPTURE
READING
John 19.28–29 After this, when Jesus knew that all was now finished, he said (in order to fulfil the scripture), 'I am thirsty.' A jar full of sour wine was standing there. So they put a sponge full of the wine on a branch of hyssop and held it to his mouth.

REFLECTION This word from the cross speaks of real human need. The most basic need of all, in the heat of the sun, and racked by pain, Jesus cries out 'I thirst', I am thirsty, give me a drink. They reach up with a sponge dipped in vinegar and gall. It's the last thing he wanted.

The hand in this image seems to capture this desperate thirst, it is dried up and desiccated, and the scratches are like spikes of gorse, echoing the crown of thorns, hard and dry and painful. Hands that flung stars into space, to cruel nails surrendered. There is an aridity and dryness in this hand that cries out 'I thirst'. He who is the 'living water bubbling up' for others to find life, he, is thirsty, and he expresses that need.

They offered Jesus vinegar and gall, a crude anaesthetic, better to be 'out of your head', to avoid the pain. We do the same with alcohol or drugs, they offer a temporary oblivion, but with lessening effect and leave us diminished. Shopping is another alternative for some. There are so many things that we think we want in life, consumer products to pamper and comfort us, luxuries to build up our self-esteem, so many inessentials that crowd in on us. They camouflage our real needs, and leave us dissatisfied. Jesus refused the distraction, preferring to feel real need rather than false comfort.

A child's deepest needs are constantly changing. Children need unconditional love, to learn basic trust, boundaries to discover inner discipline, and a growing freedom to become more autonomous. As adults we may need to fill in the gaps where some of our childhood needs were unmet. We still need love and purpose in our lives.

But we don't like to be in need, to be needy, we prefer to live from a position of strength and ability, we like to be self-reliant. And some of us need to be needed! We can test our relationships for mutuality, for the extent to which we both give and receive. Jesus lived a life of generous giving, he poured himself out for others. But he was not afraid to name and know his own real needs. He was not afraid to ask for help. In this cry from the cross, 'I thirst', we see his willingness to receive, and to be needy.

In a world of competence, this hand can encourage us to acknowledge our real needs, our incompetence at times, and to receive.

SILENCE   Let's take into this next time of reflection our own real needs, and try to sift out the many competing desires and wants. And allow Jesus' hand of real need to hold them all.

MUSIC   *A time of meditation*

FINAL PRAYER   **Gracious God,**
you know our deepest needs.
Help us to hear them too
amid the clamouring voices of
want and desire.
We thirst for your
unconditional love;
help us to receive you now.
Amen.

Concluding with

Into your hands, O Lord, I commend my spirit
For you have redeemed me, O Lord God of truth.

PARADISE

– mending our brokenness

Unexpected generosity that brings out the best in us

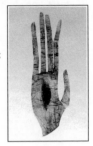

SCRIPTURE
READING
Luke 23.39–43 One of the criminals who were hanged there kept deriding him and saying, 'Are you not the Messiah? Save yourself and us!' But the other rebuked him, saying, 'Do you not fear God, since you are under the same sentence of condemnation? And we indeed have been condemned justly, for we are getting what we deserve for our deeds, but this man has done nothing wrong.' Then he said, 'Jesus, remember me when you come into your kingdom.' He replied, 'Truly I tell you, today you will be with me in Paradise.'

REFLECTION This word from the cross reaches out to one of the thieves who were crucified with Jesus. It's a promise, 'Today you will be with me in paradise.' Suffering so often drives us into isolation, takes us into ourselves, like a wounded animal we withdraw from others. But in this amazing encounter, Jesus reaches out with words of hope. His words embrace the thief in a promise of eternity.

Jake Lever described how this hand was almost discarded, it was so lacerated and damaged it seemed good for nothing! In the Far East they have a wonderful history of fine porcelain, and when some is accidentally broken, instead of trying to do an invisible repair, they do just the opposite. They gild the break, to draw attention to it, to incorporate its brokenness into its beauty. Here we see a hand that has been damaged and broken, but where the fractures have been healed in gold.

This image suggested paradise to me, the white background is like silence, it seems a little detached, cooler and more dispassionate. The gold repairs seem to suggest the healing of heaven! Our eyes are still drawn to the gaping wound in the hand, the dark shadow of pain and hurt, but even this seems more serene, the trauma is distant. But how can this be?

The two thieves on the cross had the choice, to reach out from the place of loving or of hurting. One mocked and despised, the other asked for Jesus to remember him. Sometimes unexpected generosity brings out the best in us; these are the glimpses of paradise. This is the gift of perspective, all this will pass, there is more than the 'now' of the difficult and painful processes of our lives, like someone who keeps their cool in a traffic jam or their humanity in a messy divorce, or a crisis at work.

But this kind of perspective is far from automatic, it doesn't come easily. Most of us find it hard to step out of the immediacy of the situation. It comes with a familiarity with silence, the practice of the presence of God, the sort of silence that Jesus knew in the wilderness. Sometimes there is an inner place, a memory of deep joy or love or peace, and we can open a 'window' in our minds to 'be' in that place, even in the most stressful of situations. This hand reminds us too that blessing sometimes comes to us in the form of unexpected generosity, from unexpected places.

And this image reminds us that Paradise is a place of real healing. Many of us try to cover up the cracks in our lives, the imperfections and the shortcomings. We try to hide the bad experiences that have happened to us, and we hope for an invisible mend that

will make it seem as if we have everything sorted
out, that we are really fine! But like Jesus we shall be
known by our scars.

SILENCE   Let's take into this time of reflection an experience
of real peace or love or joy that might become for us
a window onto Paradise. Where will we need to
choose between loving or hurting? Can we honour
our scars and allow Jesus' hand of promise to hold
them?

MUSIC   *A time of meditation*

FINAL PRAYER   **Lord Jesus,**
bring us to the place of inner healing
through the practice of your presence.
Open to us
deep wells of silence,
windows into Paradise,
the gift of perspective,
that we may bring to you
our deepest wounds
and find them
gilded in your glory.
Amen.

Concluding with

Into your hands, O Lord, I commend my spirit
For you have redeemed me, O Lord God of truth.

IT IS FINISHED

– honest endings

*Recognizing death and what
has been accomplished*

SCRIPTURE
READING
John 19.30 When Jesus had received the wine, he said, 'It is finished.' Then he bowed his head and gave up his spirit.

REFLECTION The next word from the cross – it is finished, the horror is over, it is accomplished, the work is done, 'consumatum est'. In the eyes of the world this is the moment of absolute failure, but in the purposes of God this is the consummation of an act of unconditional love for the world. Not just that his suffering was over, not just that his life was ending, the Greek word here, *tetelestai*, is a strong, triumphant word, *'It is accomplished', 'it is complete'*.

You can see the wood of the cross behind this hand; the pale skin, though hurt and pierced, has a strength about it, a serenity, an acceptance. The lacerations extend beyond the hand, across the wood, Jesus is holding more than just his own hurts and pain; he is holding the hurt and pain of the world, of humanity. This is not simply the story of one man's agony and death, this is about all of us.

Christians speak of Jesus taking all our sins to the cross and accepting the punishment for them on our behalf. In taking our flesh, identifying himself with us completely in his incarnation, in taking the worst and giving the best, Jesus has accomplished everything.

In the hospital the doctors fight for every moment of life for the patient, death is seen as a failure. We sometimes undergo painful and intrusive treatment to stave off death for a few days longer. Here it is so different. Here, death comes as the completion of a life lived to the full, here death comes as a friend. 'And thou most kind and gentle death, waiting to hush our latest breath, thou leadest home the child of God, and Christ himself that way has trod.'

Hospices have reminded us of the possibility of a 'good death', of being able to let go into the ultimate healing of heaven. We sometimes speak of winning or losing the battle against cancer. The real accomplishment may be the willing acceptance of the disintegration, letting go into death, to find the deeper integration in the depths of God's love.

Sometimes we may be called on to suffer for the sake of another person, more often we will have to endure the consequences of another's action. In this hand perhaps we can be encouraged to hold that hurt without letting it distort us, in the confidence that in some way we are held in the redemptive suffering of Christ.

SILENCE   Let's take into this sixth time of reflection an honesty about our own mortality, that we might be completed, accomplished in this hand.

MUSIC   *A time of meditation*

FINAL PRAYER   **Gracious God,**
accomplish in us your purposes,
complete in us your work of healing love,
that though we walk through the valley

**of the shadow of death
we may find you,
one step ahead of us,
leading us home.
Amen.**

Concluding with

Into your hands, O Lord, I commend my spirit
For you have redeemed me, O Lord God of truth.

INTO YOUR HANDS
I COMMEND MY
SPIRIT

– trusting in the darkness

*Going on when all seems
hopeless*

SCRIPTURE
READING
Luke 23.45–49 It was now about noon, and darkness came over the
whole land until three in the afternoon, while the
sun's light failed; and the curtain of the temple was
torn in two. Then Jesus, crying with a loud voice,
said, 'Father, into your hands I commend my spirit.'
Having said this, he breathed his last. When the
centurion saw what had taken place, he praised
God and said, 'Certainly this man was innocent.' And
when all the crowds who had gathered there for this
spectacle saw what had taken place, they returned
home, beating their breasts. But all his acquain-
tances, including the women who had followed him
from Galilee, stood at a distance, watching these
things.

REFLECTION The last word from the cross – 'Father, into your
hands I commend my spirit.' The last breath of Jesus,
the last movement of a terrible execution, and there
is darkness over the whole earth.

In this image we see the overwhelming darkness of
death as it extinguishes the Light of the World. This
image is hard to see, you have to stop and peer and
allow your eyes to get used to the darkness. This is the
darkest place, the 'valley of the shadow of death'. But
look, we can see in the gloom, two hands side by side,
extended to hold and support. One hand has a glimmer
of gold, the faintest outline of a wound. The Father's

hands now bear the wounds of the Son, the agony of the cross is now taken into the heart of God.

These words have become familiar in the late evening office of Compline, 'into your hands I commend my spirit' – my spirit – the spark of life that makes each one of us unique, the golden thread that is our personality, our essence, our soul. Even in the darkness of death there is the glimmer of gold, the possibility of eternity.

Each night as children we face the darkness, the unknown horrors under the bed, we let go into sleep, and the Compline prayers help us to face the fears and to trust in the coming light of morning. As adults we rehearse the possibility of death, what if I don't wake up again in the morning?

It is death that Jesus now faces, after all the passion, the words, of forgiveness, of despair and need, of promise and relationship, now there are words of trust and letting go into the darkness.

There are times when we can only see the darkness, the times of depression and sadness in our lives, times when we can do nothing else but walk on into the darkness where there is no light to guide us. Those are the 'plod on' moments, when all we can do is to take the next step.

These two hands look almost like companions walking together, Jesus our companion walks the path before us. When we come to our own last words, to face the darkness for ourselves, this image can help us to see that darkness as the place of encounter, because Jesus has been here before us.

And with all the 'little deaths' that we face, the critical operation, the dreaded meeting, the hopeless situation, these are the hands that will hold us. 'And underneath are the everlasting arms.' God reaches out to us, to catch us when we fall, to hold us when we die; to fold us into his eternal love.

SILENCE   Let's take into this last time of reflection that sense of committing our spirit to God, that spark of life that makes us each special and different, and so to find the strength for some of those 'plod on' moments, in this hand.

MUSIC   *A time of meditation*

FINAL PRAYER   **Gracious God,**
your hands now bear the wounds,
your heart now holds the agony
of that appalling cross.
Hold us in your everlasting arms
as we face the little deaths of daily life
to find you there beside us,
light in our darkest night.
Amen.

Concluding with

Into your hands, O Lord, I commend my spirit
For you have redeemed me, O Lord God of truth.

I AM THE RESURRECTION

– living with scars

Honouring the past as we break through into new patterns of life

SCRIPTURE READING
John 11.17–27 When Jesus arrived, he found that Lazarus had already been in the tomb for four days. Now Bethany was near Jerusalem, some two miles away, and many of the Jews had come to Martha and Mary to console them about their brother. When Martha heard that Jesus was coming, she went and met him, while Mary stayed at home. Martha said to Jesus, 'Lord, if you had been here, my brother would not have died. But even now I know that God will give you whatever you ask of him.' Jesus said to her, 'Your brother will rise again.' Martha said to him, 'I know that he will rise again in the resurrection on the last day.' Jesus said to her, 'I am the resurrection and the life. Those who believe in me, even though they die, will live, and everyone who lives and believes in me will never die. Do you believe this?' She said to him, 'Yes, Lord, I believe that you are the Messiah, the Son of God, the one coming into the world.'

REFLECTION This was the first of Jake Lever's prints that I ever encountered, it spoke to me powerfully, and the conversations that it triggered have led to the emergence of this book. For me it is the hand of Christ in the dawning of the resurrection. It seems to beckon through the darkness, calling to us, 'come', it is an invitation to a life that has been transfigured, glorified, made new.

The hand is like a candle flame, fragile and flickering in the darkness, a space that has been opened, through which to glimpse the glory beyond. The hand of life is marked with the experience of death, it is still scarred and marked by the scourge and nails. There is a hint of the red-brown clay (known as 'bole') underneath the gold leaf, a suggestion of pain and bloodshed. This was a costly light to hold, a hard path to tread.

This is no superhero or cartoon character who springs at once to life, as if by magic, unmarked by disaster. The resurrection and the life honours the reality of the past, the experiences that have brought us to this place. This is not simply a happy ending, where all the wrongs are righted; this is a new thing, a new and unprecedented beginning.

These moments of transfiguration, of epiphany, where the glory of God is able to shine through, just for a moment, are moments that cannot be predicted or grasped or attained. They are unpredictable, pure gift, by the grace of God, gifts that allow us to see everything else in a new light. This hand reminds me of some of the 'thin places', like Iona or Holy Island, Bardsey, where the fabric of heaven and earth come so close, and the glory can sometimes be glimpsed.

When things go wrong for us we are sometimes tempted to try to leave it all behind us, to draw a line, try to forget it and move on. It can happen in relationship, moving from partner to partner, but never dealing with the real issues. It happened for George Best after his liver transplant, he just went back to the booze. We carry our past with us, and our past mistakes will keep repeating themselves unless we can face them honestly.

In this hand we can see that the past has been fully lived, the scars can be recognized, even celebrated,

not covered up. And if we can face our woundedness, and find healing in that honesty, we will be able
to draw strength from our scars as we break through
into new patterns of life.

SILENCE   Let's take into this time of reflection God's invitation
to see through the everyday reality of our lives to the
glory that lies beyond. Let's offer our own hurts and
scars, our past, to be taken with us, transfigured into
the new life that is waiting for us.

MUSIC   *A time of meditation*

FINAL PRAYER   **Gracious God,
we glimpse the glory of your love,
unexpected light
beckoning us through the darkness,
inviting us to see with different eyes
the possibility of resurrection,
transfigured in the stuff of every day.
Call us now to follow you
into your new life.
Amen.**

Concluding with

Into your hands, O Lord, I commend my spirit
For you have redeemed me, O Lord God of truth.

PENTECOST
Dancing and Risking

Jester Hands
Stretching Our Potential

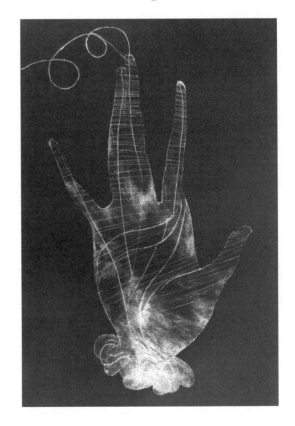

INTRODUCTION

In 2006 Jake Lever was commissioned to be artist-
in-residence at the tiny historic pilgrimage church
at Hailes in Gloucestershire and he spent a year
working with local people in the church, village
and school to develop an installation of Jester hands.
He created hundreds of images displayed in unlikely
places all over the church and celebrated in a
wonderful summer weekend of creative art and
spirituality. The Jester hands are in the tradition of
the Holy Fool. Fools for Christ often employ shock-
ing, unconventional behaviour to challenge accepted
norms, deliver prophecies or to mask their piety.
Jake wanted them to be playful and provocative
images.

In beginning to work with the images I found that
their silver form on a blue background gave them a
timeless almost cosmic feel. They connected for me
with the work of the Holy Spirit, not simply in the
gifts or fruit of the Spirit, but in some of the less
familiar modes of operation.

Delight explores the playful dance of the Sprit in
creation, the delight that God takes in us, in our
freedom to become who we truly are. **Thread** shows
us the Spirit as the divine weaver who works with
the thread of our lives to weave our mistakes into
the tapestry of creation. **Emergence** takes a very
different perspective, is hardly recognizable as a
hand, and helps us as we wrestle with the emerging
church, to discern familiar realities in unfamiliar
patterns. **Risk** sees the Spirit as the element of free
will, divine chance at the heart of creation that

allows for mutation, evolution, and the emergence of new possibilities. **Abundance** shares the gift of the Spirit in pouring abundant life, life in all its fullness, on us, overflowing generosity and grace in unexpected places. **Paradox** reveals the Spirit as leading us into all truth, in the mystery of God. It is about the transcendence of opposites, the holding together of impossible contradictions.

DELIGHT

– the dance of change

*To be alive is to move and change,
to be creative, co-creators with
God*

OPENING PRAYER Holy Spirit of God,
dancing and risking,
stretching our potential,
be present to us now
in the energy of our becoming.
Amen.

SCRIPTURE
READING
Proverbs 8.22–31

The LORD created me at the beginning of his work,
the first of his acts of long ago.
Ages ago I was set up,
at the first, before the beginning of the earth.
When there were no depths I was brought forth,
when there were no springs abounding with water.
Before the mountains had been shaped,
before the hills, I was brought forth –
when he had not yet made earth and fields,
or the world's first bits of soil.
When he established the heavens, I was there,
when he drew a circle on the face of the deep,
when he made firm the skies above,
when he established the fountains of the deep,
when he assigned to the sea its limit,
so that the waters might not transgress his command,
when he marked out the foundations of the earth,
then I was beside him, like a master worker;
and I was daily his delight,
rejoicing before him always,
rejoicing in his inhabited world
and delighting in the human race.

REFLECTION   The blue-black of the background gives luminosity to the silver of this hand. The ruff hints at the clowning, the holy foolishness of God. There is movement, playfulness, delight, a game of catch, a cradling. But what does the hand hold?

It's like a ball of string or tangled fishing line, and with infinite patience God holds and gently untangles, with us, the knots and mess we have made.

It is like an egg, cradled gently: 'You hold me in the hollow of your hand.' It is like the universe, as in the children's song 'He's got the whole world in his hand'. It's like the orbit of our planet, traversing millions of miles, yet known and held: 'You discern my paths; you encompass me behind, before' (Psalm 139).

The passage from Proverbs informs the image, speaking of Holy Wisdom present with God in creation. I love the final verses, of God delighting and rejoicing in both Wisdom and in the world in creation. The Hebrew word for delight, *Sachaq*, means to laugh, to sport, to play, to sing, to dance, to jest.

So much of our tradition has presented a God of majesty and power, to be approached with awe, fear and trembling. But here we are invited to see God in creation, delighting and rejoicing, dancing, jesting.

We can have a similarly staid picture of the holy Trinity. But the Greek word for the relationship of Father, Son and Holy Spirit means 'to dance around one another in relationship', *perichoresis* – *peri* meaning around, and *choreio* to dance. Just like Wisdom playing and delighting around God in creation.

It is the sort of life that Jesus spoke of, his purpose, inviting us to share in that delight and have life, life in all its fullness. He promised that the Holy Spirit would set us free, leading us into abundant life.

The hand cradles, in an open and free caress. It is not constraining or controlling; we are held but not held on to. We have the freedom to be who we are, to become who we shall be. Like good parents supporting and releasing their children to become people in their own right. *'Your children are not your children,'* said Kahlil Gibran, *'They are the sons and daughters of Life's longing for itself.'*

And this freedom extends to the whole of creation. The process of evolution suggests a willingness of God to allow creation to move and to change, to become whatever it will become. And God delights in it, especially in the duck-billed platypus, the flamingo and the three-toed sloth!

MUSIC AND SILENCE
In this time of quiet reflection we think of our own experiences. Are we able to delight in our lives, to be playful, to laugh, to dance? What would need to change in us to allow this to happen more often?

INVOCATION
O Holy Wisdom,
darling and delight in creation,
in your infinite gentleness
cradle our humanity,
fragile shell of our potential,
the complex knotted tangle of our lives,
impossible mess and muddle
of loves, wants and needs;
in your open embrace,
disturb and awaken us
with freedom to be and become
'Life's longing';
in the energy of your rejoicing,
infect us with your laughter,
intrigue us with your play,
gather us in the choreography of your
abundant delight!

We bring to God the tangles that we face in our own
lives, the knotted relationships, hardened hearts,
hurtful words and actions, situations that seem too
hard to undo.

Cantor: In your infinite gentleness
All: Cradle our humanity

We bring to God all that is fragile and vulnerable in
us, where we have been wounded, where we have
known weakness, where we are close to breaking
point.

Cantor: In your infinite gentleness
All: Cradle our humanity

We bring to God all that is constrained in us, the
disapproving voices, the critical eyes, the cynical
thoughts, all that prevents us from delighting in our
lives.

Cantor: In your infinite gentleness
All: Cradle our humanity

And because God delights in us, we delight in the
wonder of creation, the beauty of the natural world,
the immensity of the universe and our particular
calling to enjoy and care for it.

Cantor: Disturb and awaken us
All: With freedom to be and become

We delight in the variety and peculiarity of the
human race, welcoming difference and diversity in
the abundance of our living.

Cantor: Disturb and awaken us
All: With freedom to be and become

We delight in your presence, as we learn to play, to dance, to laugh and to rejoice. Free the child in us to be and to become who we truly are.

Cantor: Disturb and awaken us
All: With freedom to be and become

PRAYERS OF *A time of open prayer when we can bring to God*
INTERCESSION *people and situations that we care about*

After each intercession
Let us pray to the Lord
Lord have mercy

CLOSING PRAYER **God of all delighting,
your laughter fills the universe
with pleasure in creation;
divine foolishness,
holy Jester,
eternal dance,
you touch the child in each of us
to open eyes of wonder,
hearts of welcome,
lives of innocence;
we trust you with our selves:
surprise us with your joy.
Amen.**

THREAD
– the weft of life

*Weaving the threads of
life together – our mistakes –
into a new future*

OPENING PRAYER

Holy Spirit of God,
dancing and risking,
stretching our potential,
be present to us now
in the energy of our becoming.
Amen.

SCRIPTURE
READING
Genesis 50.17–21

'I beg you, forgive the crime of your brothers and the
wrong they did in harming you.' Joseph wept when
they spoke to him. Then his brothers also wept, fell
down before him, and said, 'We are here as your
slaves.' But Joseph said to them, 'Do not be afraid!
Am I in the place of God? Even though you intended
to do harm to me, God intended it for good, in order
to preserve a numerous people, as he is doing today.
So have no fear.'

REFLECTION

There is incredible tension in this hand, held in the
elaborate arch of the wrist and fingers, yet a beauti-
ful fluidity of movement, like the gesture of an
Indian classical dancer. The Jester's ruff adds to this
impression of a dancer whose effortless grace
belies the long hours of hard training that have
made it all possible. The elaborate pose of the
fingers suggests symbolic meaning, a hidden depth
to the movement.

Thread coils through the air and is held delicately between thumb and finger. Despite the tension of the hand, the thread is not held taught in a straight line, but is free to loop and coil in its own way. The loops suggest the cycles of our lives, the repeated patterns, the returning to where we began. If this is the hand of God, perhaps we are the thread, to be woven into the warp and weft of life?

The single thread held with such delicacy of touch reminds us that we are known and cherished as individuals, that God numbers the hairs on our head. But our lives only make sense within the strands of other lives. Each of us also belongs in the larger picture of family and friends, community and church, in the corporate fabric of all humanity. God cares about the individual pattern of each of our lives, as well as the larger picture of human relating. This is complex thread work, needed if we are to pass a camel through the eye of a needle!

It is good that this is God's work not just ours!

As we look more deeply into the texture of the hand, we discover that it is made of the same thread. We are intimately and intrinsically linked with our creator: part of our thread is divine, soul, spirit, essence, image of God.

The opposing thumb and finger also remind us of our amazing ability as human beings. Our hands can grip and manipulate, can invent and make, we wield incredible power, for good or ill, because of this single anatomical development.

One of the earliest human skills to be developed was the ability to weave threads to make cloth. It has been a potent motif used in many ways to describe our relationship with God. The pattern of perfect creation is held in the mind of the Divine Weaver, who involves us in the process of creation, honouring

our choices and decisions, working with our
freedom, incorporating our mistakes, to fashion
an even more glorious tapestry.

At the end of the Joseph story the brothers are filled
with remorse because of the way that they have
abused Joseph. Their jealousy led them to attack him,
sell him into slavery, and to deceive their father. But
Joseph reassures them, 'Even though you intended
harm to me, God intended it for good.' God's
unwavering intention is to bring good out of evil, life
out of death, love out of hatred. God invites us to
weave this same transformative pattern with him.

MUSIC AND   We take into the silence the thread of our story, look-
SILENCE   ing back on the patterns of our life, the choices we
have made, and the consequences of that choosing.
We look to discern the Weaver's hand in our shaping.

INVOCATION   O Divine Weaver,
you gift us with the thread of your spirit,
charged with your image and essence,
life of your Life,
love of your Love;
you invite us to see in your mind's eye
Love's pattern and plan,
our place in creation,
our life in your loom;
within the warp and weft of our belonging,
redeem the fabric of our lives,
crafting sense and beauty
from freedom's shame and sorrow;
now as evolution's gift of dexterous grip propels us
and we weave the very stuff of life,
atom and genome,
to unknown ends,
guard and guide our delicate thread
through the eye of the needle
to the glory of your heavenly tapestry.

PRAYERS OF
RECOGNITION
We bring to God the times we have lost sight of the tapestry of love, and thought only of our own wants and desires. We remember now our connectedness.

Cantor: Life of your Life
All: Love of your Love

We bring to God the mistakes and choices that have marred and damaged the web of our relationships, with friends and with strangers. We remember now that we belong.

Cantor: Life of your Life
All: Love of your Love

We bring to God the awesome power of our hands, our inventiveness and imagination, used with insufficient maturity or thought. We remember now that we are your children.

Cantor: Life of your Life
All: Love of your Love

And because we are held in the warp and weft of Love, we freely offer the thread of our life to be woven in a pattern that is not our own, as part of an eternal picture, trusting to the hand of the Weaver.

Cantor: Guard and guide our delicate thread
All: Through the eye of the needle

We freely offer the thread of our love to welcome and weave in the stranger, to embrace and support those in need.

Cantor: Guard and guide our delicate thread
All: Through the eye of the needle

We freely offer the thread of our ability and intelligence as we push back the frontiers of our knowledge, for the good of all.

Cantor: Guard and guide our delicate thread
All: Through the eye of the needle

PRAYERS OF *A time of open prayer when we can bring to God*
INTERCESSION *people and situations that we care about*

After each intercession
Let us pray to the Lord
Lord have mercy

CONCLUDING **O God the weaver of life,**
PRAYER   **hold in your hand the single thread of our being**
with infinite patience and care;
invite us to find our place
within the fabric of all humanity;
gently repair and restore us
with your endless ingenuity,
incorporating our knotted muddles
to greater glory.
Amen.

EMERGENCE

– the surfacing of
the new

*Discerning the authentic
life of the Spirit at the
leading edge*

OPENING PRAYER   Holy Spirit of God,
dancing and risking,
stretching our potential,
be present to us now
in the energy of our becoming.
Amen.

SCRIPTURE
READING
1 Samuel 3. 1–10

The boy Samuel was ministering to the LORD under Eli. The word of the LORD was rare in those days; visions were not widespread. At that time Eli, whose eyesight had begun to grow dim so that he could not see, was lying down in his room; the lamp of God had not yet gone out, and Samuel was lying down in the temple of the LORD, where the ark of God was. Then the LORD called, 'Samuel! Samuel!' and he said, 'Here I am!' and ran to Eli, and said, 'Here I am, for you called me.' But he said, 'I did not call; lie down again.' So he went and lay down. The LORD called again, 'Samuel!' Samuel got up and went to Eli, and said, 'Here I am, for you called me.' But he said, 'I did not call, my son; lie down again.' Now Samuel did not yet know the LORD, and the word of the LORD had not yet been revealed to him. The LORD called Samuel again, a third time. And he got up and went to Eli, and said, 'Here I am, for you called me.' Then Eli perceived that the LORD was calling the boy. Therefore Eli said to Samuel, 'Go, lie down; and if he calls you, you shall say, "Speak, LORD, for your servant is listening."' So Samuel went and lay down in his place. Now the LORD came and stood there, calling as before, 'Samuel! Samuel!' And Samuel said, 'Speak, for your servant is listening.'

REFLECTION   There is so much that cannot be seen in this image! If you stop and let your eyes adjust to the darkness you can begin to see some hints of what more might be there. This is still a hand, but seen from a different angle, lit from below – we often only see from one perspective. There is a thread, the suggestion of the connection between the divine touch and the thread of our lives, but this seems a very different kind of hand.

This is what happens when we move into new territory. We lose our bearings; we no longer recognize the familiar forms. This hand shows us a new future emerging, it speaks of the leading edge, but so little can be seen here.

In the church there are new patterns emerging to respond to a postmodern world. We hear of 'fresh expressions', network church, liquid church, café church, a changing church for a changing world. But can we trust the leading edge? Are we simply accommodating a culture instead of challenging it?

In family life and in human relationships there are new patterns emerging. Marriage has been abandoned by many, there are new sexualities, transgendered people, a fluidity about who we are. Children are now growing up in a huge variety of relationships. The future will become even more complex as the possibilities of genetic manipulation become even more developed. How will we love, and live in this emerging future?

In the environment we are also seeing a very different future unfolding, with global warming threatening fundamental change in our weather systems. How will this affect the water levels, the temperature, the relationship between rich and poor? How will we adapt and change to meet this new future?

In these fast-changing situations we may be tempted to revert to a default setting for so many people of faith, to be against change, almost on principle, and to resist it at all costs. Like the Amish community, we try to hold on to a fabled golden age.

It was the same for Eli. He could no longer see clearly; the word of the Lord was rare in those times. Fresh eyes are needed, new ways of seeing required for changed times. The old days were good, but new days lie ahead. God calls Samuel, but the youngster lacks experience, and fails to recognize God's call. In the end, young and old worked together to make the connection, for a new ministry to emerge.

It is much more difficult to walk forwards into an unknown future, where the familiar landmarks have disappeared, than to stay in the past; but we have no choice if we believe that God's Holy Spirit is leading us into all truth, into situations that we cannot yet understand.

So as we peer into the image, can we begin to see the thread of continuity with what we have known? You can just begin to trace the outline of the fingers, hardly visible; yet they meet and match the pattern of the thread, through time, in the act of creation. It is almost like a high-wire act, where balance and poise are needed if one is to walk what John Bell calls 'faith's tightrope'.

MUSIC AND In this time of quiet reflection we think of the cer-
SILENCE tainties we have known in our faith and in our lives, and of how we have needed to change and accommodate new patterns. We look for the continuity of love undergirding it all.

INVOCATION   Elusive Word,
              unfamiliar and unrecognized
              in the shifting scenes
              at the leading edge of our emerging future;
              our eyes grow dim, our vision rare,
              faith and love and life lose their bearings
              in unfamiliar territory;
              we long for home, fabled golden age,
              but find it empty,
              you are gone.
              Speak, Lord, your servant is listening.
              How will we love and live when all is changing?
              Your lamp has not yet gone out,
              fresh eyes peer into the darkness;
              could this be you,
              a new perspective,
              your voice,
              calling us to attend?
              Speak, Lord, your servant is listening.

              Continuities emerge,
              love traverses generations,
              hope awakens fresh expression,
              we walk faith's tightrope
              unsteadily.

PRAYERS OF   We bring to God the changes we find hard to
RECOGNITION   understand or accept, in our church, our family,
              in ourselves.

              Cantor: Speak, Lord
              All: Your servant is listening

              We bring to God our uncertainty as we move into
              unfamiliar territory, our fears and our anxieties about
              how we will fit in to new patterns.

              Cantor: Speak, Lord
              All: Your servant is listening

We bring to God the big changes that we face in the
wider world, of climate, of economics, of global
powers.

Cantor: Speak, Lord
All: Your servant is listening

And because God's love is steadfast, we renew our
confidence in ourselves as people called and graced
by God to face uncertain days with hope.

Cantor: Here I am
All: For you called me

We renew our commitment to the future as a place
and time hallowed by God for our flourishing.

Cantor: Here I am
All: For you called me

We renew our vocation to walk faith's tightrope
affirming for all that you are there to encounter us
as we embrace the future.

Cantor: Here I am
All: For you called me

PRAYERS OF   *A time of open prayer when we can bring to God*
INTERCESSION   *people and situations that we care about*

After each intercession
Let us pray to the Lord
Lord have mercy

CLOSING PRAYER   **Speak, Lord, for your servant is listening**
amidst the clamour of changing times,
the bewildering complexity of new worlds
**   emerging.**

Your persistent call goes unrecognized at first,
so call and call again,
awaken us
to the constant thread of your presence,
continuity of love,
unwavering hope,
resolute faith,
in ways we cannot even imagine.
Amen.

RISK
– the freedom of creation

Improvisation and mutation where
all is risked for love to be free

OPENING PRAYER Holy Spirit of God,
dancing and risking,
stretching our potential,
be present to us now
in the energy of our becoming.
Amen.

SCRIPTURE The angel said to her, 'The Holy Spirit will come
READING upon you, and the power of the Most High will
Luke 1.35–38 overshadow you; therefore the child to be born will
be holy; he will be called Son of God. And now, your
relative Elizabeth in her old age has also conceived a
son; and this is the sixth month for her who was said
to be barren. For nothing will be impossible with
God.' Then Mary said, 'Here am I, the servant of the
Lord; let it be with me according to your word.' Then
the angel departed from her.

REFLECTION This hand is full of movement; it seems to soar
through the heavens, the blue-black of the background gives a vast scale, the hand of God in
creation bringing the universe into being? Our eyes
are drawn to the star in the palm of the hand,
stigmata-like, the mark of the cross, 'Hands that
flung stars into space, to cruel nails surrendered'.
The star-wound is the strongest point of energy in
the image, redemptive suffering is the costly mark of
creative love, giving life to the whole.

Our attention is drawn to the fingertips; specks of light hint at the immensity of the creation. The fingers are curved, quirky; they suggest an originality that is far from 'perfect' in a conventional sense, yet graceful and animated. It reminds me of a family trait, a curved finger that is repeated down the generations. It is a particular genetic pattern and points us to the slow process of evolution, where naturally occurring mutations allow species to adapt to changing environments. It is not just we humans who have free will, for the whole created order is free to become what it will. Sometimes these mutations will be beneficial, sometimes harmful, but if we are to live, the risk must be taken.

At every level within the continuing story of our creation, the Holy Spirit is the energy that holds us in being. We are wrong to speak of creation in the past tense, for God is, even now, creating the heavens and the earth. The Holy Spirit gives the freedom to evolve, even at the subatomic level, where randomness, chaos, is contained, but not tamed.

Micheal O Siadhail's poem 'Hail Madam Jazz' likens the improvisation in jazz music to this work of the Spirit. Musicians hold the knowledge of the melody, the 'original' tune, but they are free to depart from it, to improvise, while remaining in relationship to it. Such freedom is inherently risky, so much can go wrong, but the risk is essential for life.

The story of God's people throughout the Bible is of a God who chooses to take incredible risks; to trust weak and fallible human beings with things that really matter. This is never more true than in the story of the incarnation, when the Word becomes flesh, a young woman is overshadowed by the Holy Spirit, there are risks all round. Will she accept this gift? Will she survive as an unmarried mother? As the child becomes an adult, the human face of God, how will we respond to a love that sets us free? What happens when we exercise our freedom, to crucify?

We prefer to minimize risk, we take out insurance policies, install burglar alarms, surround our children with sometimes stifling layers of protection. In our self-made security we may lose sight of the God who chooses to 'risk all for love'. In St Patrick's Cathedral in Dublin there is a hole in a door where in 1492, in the midst of a feud, Gerald Fitzgerald wanted to make peace. He cut a hole in the door and 'chanced his arm', putting his own arm through, to show that his offer of reconciliation was genuine. He put himself at his opponent's mercy, he risked all for peace.

The mark of the nail in this image brings out the story of the cross on a cosmic scale. It doesn't labour the woundedness, the pain or the hurt; instead, it points to the bigger picture, the vision, the stars. So it points us to the universal pattern of God setting us free to risk all for love.

And even when, in the risky freedom of love, we sometimes choose the way of darkness, of hurt and of harm, God does not give up on us, but continues to believe in our goodness, continues to offer us new possibilities, new opportunities to choose light and life. God continues to believe in us and dares to risk all for love, again and again.

MUSIC AND SILENCE In this time of quiet reflection we think of our security, our attempts to minimize risk. We think too of the risks that we have taken in our lives, and why we have taken them.

INVOCATION O Spirit of risk and chance,
energy in every particle and atom,
holding us in being in this and every moment,
you set your whole creation free to move and change;

subtle jazz, you improvise upon your theme –
mutation in the face of each new challenge –
adapting and adopting for survival,
evolution's gift of becoming.
You set us free from deadening security,
to risk freedom's fall;
from stifling certainty, to questions, doubt and faith!
You risk all for love,
empty yourself that we might be full,
chance your arm that we might learn to trust,
offer your hands, even to nails,
open your heart, even to breaking.
No depths unharrowed,
no darkness forsaken,
you encompass all,
redeeming our costly choices,
overshadowing our humanity,
with your invitation
to risk all for love, again.

PRAYERS OF
RECOGNITION
We bring to you our longing for security and safety,
our insurances, and protections, and the walls we
sometimes erect around ourselves.

Cantor: You encompass all
All: Redeeming our costly choices

We bring to you the times of anxiety and fear, when
we have turned away from your call to risk all for love.

Cantor: You encompass all
All: Redeeming our costly choices

We bring to you the choices we have made that have
led to hurt and unhappiness for others.

Cantor: You encompass all
All: Redeeming our costly choices

And because God does call us again and again, give us courage to break down the walls of our fearfulness and to chance our arm, to reach out with hands of peace.

Cantor: Overshadow our humanity
All: **To risk all for love, again**

Help us to dare to believe that nothing is impossible for you, to respond to your call, to step into the unknown with you.

Cantor: Overshadow our humanity
All: **To risk all for love, again**

Help us to hear the subtle jazz of your creative love in all the changes and chances of our lives and to embrace them.

Cantor: Overshadow our humanity
All: **To risk all for love, again**

PRAYERS OF INTERCESSION *A time of open prayer when we can bring to God people and situations that we care about*

After each intercession
Let us pray to the Lord
Lord have mercy

CLOSING PRAYER **Holy Spirit of God,**
overshadow us with your love,
help us to say with Mary,
'Here I am;
let it be with me
according to your Word.'
Inspire us with your promise
that nothing will be impossible for you;
help us to dare to risk all for love.
Amen.

ABUNDANCE

– the overflowing of love

Surprised by joy, profligate generosity in unexpected places

OPENING PRAYER

Holy Spirit of God,
dancing and risking,
stretching our potential,
be present to us now
in the energy of our becoming.
Amen.

SCRIPTURE
READING
1 Corinthians 1.18–25

The message about the cross is foolishness to those who are perishing, but to us who are being saved it is the power of God. For it is written, 'I will destroy the wisdom of the wise, and the discernment of the discerning I will thwart.' Where is the one who is wise? Where is the scribe? Where is the debater of this age? Has not God made foolish the wisdom of the world? For since, in the wisdom of God, the world did not know God through wisdom, God decided, through the foolishness of our proclamation, to save those who believe. For Jews demand signs and Greeks desire wisdom, but we proclaim Christ crucified, a stumbling-block to Jews and foolishness to Gentiles, but to those who are the called, both Jews and Greeks, Christ the power of God and the wisdom of God. For God's foolishness is wiser than human wisdom, and God's weakness is stronger than human strength.

REFLECTION

The Jester's ruff draws the eye, the light seems to gather, the energy shines like sunlit clouds, or nebulae in the night sky. Drawn to the light, or spinning from it, there are strands of light, threads, some curling, some straight, reaching to the fingertips, and beyond. This image speaks to me of abundant energy gathered and distributed, of empowerment, of enlightenment. All this is given focus in one strand, one life, in you? It reminds me of a prayer that speaks of God's love shining, like light from the sun, whether accepted, rejected or ignored. God loves continually, not dependent on our reaction, but because it is his being to love. In the present tense, God so loves the world that he gives his only begotten Son.

But the Jester's ruff also reminds us that the energy of love is to be found in unexpected places and people. It is not to be contained or predicted, it is always surprising. The Jester is a Holy Fool, who overturns our expectations and reminds us that the foolishness of God is wiser than the wisdom of the world, that God's weakness is stronger than human strength.

There is a long tradition of Holy Fools, like St Francis of Assisi who gave up the prosperity of his family business to embrace holy poverty. Symeon of Emesa, the patron saint of holy fools, used his foolery to hide his saintliness, made a fool of himself to avoid attention. The fool in King Lear was the one who told the truth and showed up the real foolishness in those around him.

Jesus himself overturned worldly wisdom, and his life and gospel are dismissed as foolishness by many. His abundant love embraced the unloveable, and unlovely. He trusted the untrustworthy, gave second chances to those who let him down. His foolish choices included fishermen and tax collectors, lepers and prostitutes to be his followers. His path took him into the heart of the storm, provoking the powerful

to crush him. In human eyes his ministry failed, his
supporters deserted him, the cross was a scandal.
But the light and energy of this image reminds us
that the abundance of love is to be found in surprising places and people. It is love and laughter, joy and
compassion that are really true, and not the powers
and principalities that think they rule this world.
When we are feeling crushed and constrained by the
orthodoxies of this age, it is time to play the fool,
and to dare to proclaim Christ crucified.

MUSIC AND   In this time of quiet reflection we think of the seem-
SILENCE   ing foolishness of our faith. We think of times we
have felt inadequate in the eyes of the world. And
we take confidence in the foolishness of God's love,
even for us.

INVOCATION   O Jester,
your laughter echoes through the universe,
dispelling fear, deflating ego, diffusing tension.
Foolish wisdom, gentle strength,
you overturn the tables of our worldliness,
spilling the currency of our power,
choosing to call the jokers to your pack,
to shame the wisdom of the wise,
to crumble the certainty of the strong,
enduring the thorny crown of mockery,
transforming the cross of shame
into the tree of life.
You refuse to be contained within our formulations,
to be adopted by our empires,
to be recruited to any cause,
save for your own
generous Love
shining continually
like light from the sun,

whether accepted, rejected, or ignored,
available to us
abundantly.

PRAYERS OF   We acknowledge before God the hardness of our
RECOGNITION   world, impersonal markets, multinational corpora-
tions, oppressive governments.

Cantor: Shame the wisdom of the wise
All: **Crumble the certainty of the strong**

We acknowledge before God the hardness of our
hearts, looking to our own needs, desires and
demands.

Cantor: Shame the wisdom of the wise
All: **Crumble the certainty of the strong**

We acknowledge before God all those who are over-
looked, ignored, demeaned and mocked in our
world.

Cantor: Shame the wisdom of the wise
All: **Crumble the certainty of the strong**

And because your laughter transforms us, we offer
to God the foolish gifts of mercy and forgiveness in
us, to be used to meet those who feel judged by the
world and found wanting.

Cantor: God's foolishness is wiser than human
          wisdom
All: **God's weakness stronger than human
          strength**

We offer to God our own vulnerability and weakness,
as opportunities for grace.

Cantor: God's foolishness is wiser than human wisdom

All: **God's weakness stronger than human strength**

We offer to God our sense of humour, our ability to laugh at ourselves, and at each other.

Cantor: God's foolishness is wiser than human wisdom

All: **God's weakness stronger than human strength**

PRAYERS OF   *A time of open prayer when we can bring to God*
INTERCESSION   *people and situations that we care about*

After each intercession
Let us pray to the Lord
Lord have mercy

CLOSING PRAYER   **God of love and laughter,**
undermine the wisdom of the world
with your subversive foolishness,
overturn the powers of this world
with your strength made perfect in our frailty,
open our eyes to find you in unexpected places,
surprise us with your abundant life.
Amen.

PARADOX

– transcendence of opposites

Holding together impossible contradictions to reach for the infinite

OPENING PRAYER Holy Spirit of God,
dancing and risking,
stretching our potential,
be present to us now
in the energy of our becoming.
Amen.

SCRIPTURE
READING
2 Corinthians 12.6–10

But if I wish to boast, I will not be a fool, for I will be speaking the truth. But I refrain from it, so that no one may think better of me than what is seen in me or heard from me, even considering the exceptional character of the revelations. Therefore, to keep me from being too elated, a thorn was given me in the flesh, a messenger of Satan to torment me, to keep me from being too elated. Three times I appealed to the Lord about this, that it would leave me, but he said to me, 'My grace is sufficient for you, for power is made perfect in weakness.' So, I will boast all the more gladly of my weaknesses, so that the power of Christ may dwell in me. Therefore I am content with weaknesses, insults, hardships, persecutions, and calamities for the sake of Christ; for whenever I am weak, then I am strong.

REFLECTION

This hand seems to be full of contradictions! It is drawn from the hand of a 92-year-old, you can see the arthritic swollen knuckle joints, the frailty of the fingers, bent with age, yet despite the signs of great age it is a hand that still reaches out in exploration; it reminds us of St Paul's words, 'power is made perfect in weakness'.

The image is paradoxical, at one point the hand is fully formed and detailed, even down to the finger-nails, at another it is barely complete, the palm and wrist seem to tail off into nothingness. The clusters of light draw our eyes; the blue background and the tiny pinpricks of light suggest distant stars, like maps of constellations, Orion's Belt and the Plough. The hand does not fully contain the points of light, but seems to be coming from the far distant light, reaching from the light into the darkness.

We use paradox to try to speak of things that cannot be comprehended or contained within our finite mortal comprehension; through paradox we try to express the inexpressible. 'Immortal, invisible, God only wise, in light inaccessible, hid from our eyes.' How can we understand time and eternity? How can God be both one and three persons? How can the Word become flesh, divinity take on human form?

Paradox is about the transcendence of seeming opposites. The creator of the universe sleeping in a manger, the source of all life helpless hangs upon the cross. The central paradox of the Christian faith is the incarnation, the complex interplay of spirit and flesh in the life of Jesus. How could he be both human and divine? We try to work out that same interplay in our own lives of spirit and flesh, body and soul.

The hand in this image brings this into focus as we come to face the ultimate unknown at the end of our own life. What will happen to us when our flesh can no longer contain the unique personality that is me? How can we have a 'good death', a holy death?

St Paul's answer was to hear God saying 'my grace is

sufficient for you, for power is made perfect in weakness' and to know that *'for me to live is Christ, to die is gain'.* In the image we can begin to see through the hand, it is translucent, we can see through to eternity. It is an awareness of God's grace that will hold us as we pass through the paradox of death to the life that is infinite.

MUSIC AND SILENCE   In this time of quiet reflection we think of our own mortality, 'dust you are and to dust you shall return', and of the times when we have known God's grace made perfect in our human weakness.

INVOCATION   O Paradox,
you who hold together
impossible contradictions
of Word made flesh
in time and eternity.
Child of the manger,
you hallow our humanity,
treasure in clay jars,
infinitely valued.
Crucified one,
you inhabit our mortality,
absorbing hate,
forgiving all.
Gardener of the empty tomb,
you call us by our name,
kindling our hope
of resurrection life.
Expand our horizon
with your infinite possibility,
transcend the limitations
of our human weakness
with your sufficient grace.

We bring to you the 'thorn in our flesh', our physical limitations, our need for healing, all that seems to hold us back.

Cantor: Transcend our human weakness
All: With your sufficient grace

We bring to you the impossible contradictions of our lives, the attitudes and actions that do not match our words.

Cantor: Transcend our human weakness
All: With your sufficient grace

We bring to you our fear, especially our fear of death, for ourselves and our loved ones.

Cantor: Transcend our human weakness
All: With your sufficient grace

And because your grace is sufficient for us, and your strength is made perfect in our human weakness, we offer to you ourselves, body, mind and spirit, to be held and healed, integrated and made whole.

Cantor: You call us by our name
All: Our hope of resurrection life

We offer to you our abilities, our gifts, our energies, to be directed and used, in the service of your love.

Cantor: You call us by our name
All: Our hope of resurrection life

We offer to you our faith, to be stretched, tested and re-made that we may enjoy the mystery of your paradox.

Cantor: You call us by our name
All: Our hope of resurrection life

PRAYERS OF *A time of open prayer when we can bring to God*
INTERCESSION *people and situations that we care about*

After each intercession
Let us pray to the Lord
Lord have mercy

CLOSING PRAYER **God of mystery,**
your all-sufficient grace
encompasses everything that we are.
You know us completely.
Help us to know you, to trust you, to follow you.
Bring us at the last
to live for ever in your love.
Amen.